STRANGE

OF

MYSTERY

UNEXPLAINED

STEPH YOUNG

COPYRIGHT 2019 STEPH YOUNG

ALL RIGHTS RESERVED

Introduction

Join me for some true tales of mystery, of the most cryptic kind. Who killed Sherlock Holmes' greatest fan? Was Richard Lancelyn Green killed by a rival, an assassin, or by his own hands? What happened to Colonel Shue, found dead in his car with his nipples missing? What did Neo Babson Maximus mean when he told his sister, "The answer lies in the Periodic Table," as he fled for his life through the woods? In the story of Pauline Picard, we have a missing girl, a girl who is a doppelganger, a dead girl without a head, and a dead man without a body; all of whom are mysteriously unidentified! Who killed who and why? plus many more mysterious stories...

Many of these strange and curious stories I have written about over the last few years, across a number of my previous books. They continue to intrigue me, and while some of my readers may be familiar with some of these cryptic tales, I present them once more, in much deeper format, delving more deeply into these mysterious events and the cast of characters who feature in them.... Mysteries which yearn to be solved.

Some of these tales can also be heard on my podcast on iTunes: Tales of Mystery Unexplained.

Strange Tales of Mystery Unexplained

Who doesn't love an unexplained, cryptic, and beguiling mystery?

Strange Tales of Mystery Unexplained

Table of Contents

Introduction 2
Chapter One: The Mystery Death Of Sherlock Holmes' Greatest Fan 6
Chapter Two: The Case Of Pauline Picard 17
Chapter Three: Neo Babson Maximus 24
Chapter Four: Mr. Rouse & Mr. Popper 32
Chapter Five: Strange Things In Warminster 41
Chapter Six: The Runcorn Riddle 51
Chapter Seven: The Baffling Demise Of Colonel Shue 63
Chapter Eight: The Mystery On Ilkley Moor 82
Chapter Nine: The Missing Body Parts 91
Chapter Ten: The Mystery Of The Silver Elves & The Missing Man 108
Chapter Eleven: The Strange Death Of Edgar Allan Poe 124
Chapter Twelve: Who Was The Dolocher? 132
Chapter Thirteen: The May Day Mystery 139
Chapter Fourteen: Who Was The Mysterious Showman? 153
Chapter Fifteen: The Missing Genius 165

Chapter Sixteen: Who Were He Children In The Polaroid? 182
Chapter Seventeen: What Happened To Henry Mccabe? 191
Chapter Eighteen: What Happened To David Plunkett? 207
Chapter Nineteen: The Boy In The Red Dress 211
Chapter Twenty: The Lipstick On The Dead 220
Chapter Twenty-One: The Curious Case Of Christopher Case 222
Chapter Twenty-Two: The Tale Of Jacob Mutton 230
Chapter Twenty-Three: The Last Haunting Photo 234
Chapter Twenty-Four: The Puzzle Of Charles Mccullar 241
Chapter Twenty-Five: The Wax Men The Stick Men & The Mannequins 246
Chapter Twenty-Six: The Vampyres 261
Chapter Twenty-Seven: The Children Who Disappeared Into The Mountain 265
Chapter Twenty-Eight: The Hexham Heads 274

Chapter One:

The Mystery death of Sherlock Holmes' greatest fan

Ricard Lancelyn Green was probably the foremost collector of the personal papers and materials of the great detective writer Sir Arthur Conan Doyle, the creator of Sherlock Holmes. Lancelyn Green also probably had the largest collection of memorabilia of Sherlock Holmes ever gathered too, and his death would ironically turn out to be most fitting for a plot in one of the Sherlock Holmes novels; though the solution to his death remains cryptically unsolved.

On the 24th of May 2004, Ricard Lancelyn Green was discovered dead in his home in Kensington London. A shoelace had been wound around his neck and then tightened with the handle of a wooden spoon. He had been garrotted. There was no sign of forced entry into his apartment. It almost appeared to be a locked-room mystery. Just prior to his death, Lancelyn Green had said "someone" was after him, yet his death looked more like a suicide. He was found lying on his bed, surrounded by stuffed toys and a bottle of Gin.

A graduate of Oxford University, Green had been co-author of the first extensive biography of Sir Arthur Conan Doyle, and he had also published a collection of Conan Doyle's writing that had never been put into book form before, comprising stories, essays, and personal letters. Though wealthy Mr. Green was said to be a shy man, he had often been a public speaker on his favourite topic, and at events for the Sherlock Holmes Society he would dress in the 19th Century outfit of a music hall master and perform as their Master of Ceremonies. From boyhood, Green had been fascinated with Sherlock Holmes and Doctor Watson, and he had even re-created Sherlock Holmes' fictional house 221b Baker Street in his family's attic room. In adulthood, he would publish a collection of letters that had been sent by fans of Holmes to the Abbey National Bank which sat on the site of Holme's fictional address at Baker Street. Green had an encyclopaedic knowledge of all of Conan Doyle's works and he was highly respected by other scholars in that field. He had been working for many years on a definitive Opus; a 3-volume biography of Conan Doyle, and he'd been collecting masses of material for this huge work.

After Conan Doyle's death in 1930, many of his papers, said to be worth in their millions, seemed to have vanished. Green had been searching for them for years. He needed them to complete his research for the biography. The London Times wrote that the location of these archives had become 'a mystery as tantalizing as any to unfold at 221B Baker Street.'

Green discovered that Adrian, one of Conan Doyle's children, had secreted away many of these papers in a locked room in a chateau he owned in Switzerland, with the agreement of Conan Doyle's other children. Adrian had then later, Green believed, stashed some of these papers elsewhere, without the knowledge of Conan Doyle's other children. Green was said to have alleged that Adrian was in the process of trying to sell some of these items when he died suddenly of a heart attack. Upon Adrian's death, the location of these papers became unknown. For many years, Green kept digging, following trail after false trail, wherever it led, including the time it apparently led to a Russian Princess, who it was said was not really a Princess but an expert in double-cross and deception! Finally though, Green found that the trail led to the youngest daughter of Conan Doyle, Dame Jean Doyle, a former officer in the Royal Airforce and now in her sixties, living in London. Green contacted the Dame and began to develop somewhat of a friendship with her. She invited him to her home and one day, says David Grann, staff writer for the New Yorker, who carried out the most extensive research into the death of Mr. Green for his publication 'The Devil and Sherlock Holmes,' Dame Jean showed Green a box. Inside this box were some of the papers Green had been in search of for so long. However, Green was only allowed a peep at them. Dame Jean explained that he was not allowed to take a close look at them because the items were in the midst of a family dispute. They were to be kept at a solicitor's for safe keeping, she told him. Dame Jean told Green that upon her death, they would be bequeathed to The British Library, so that all scholars would have access to them.

When Dame Jean died in 1977, Green excitedly waited for his chance to finally see the papers, examine them, and read them in The British Library. He waited and waited, but they never arrived at the Library. Imagine his horror then, when opening his newspaper one Sunday morning to discover that Dame Jean's archives were being listed by Christie's Auction House in London! They were to be sold to the highest bidder, within weeks. Lanceyln Green simply could not believe this was happening. Now, whoever had the most money, from whatever country, would be able to take them away to add to their own private collection, and he would never get the chance to see them; never be able to use them for his definitive biography that he had spent years writing. This was a disaster and a disgrace. He had to do something. So, he hurried off to Christie's as soon as it was open the following day, to see the items for himself. Here they were, tantalisingly within his grasp yet about to disappear forever. This would be the last time he would see them before they were taken and hidden away again. Not only that, but Green was certain that in this collection were the very papers he had been hunting for so many years; and, that these papers had been stolen! He told people; he knew this, because he had the proof!

In a rush to bring a halt to the auction, Green contacted members of the London Sherlock Holmes Society, where he had once been Chairman, as well as many of the most eminent scholars of Sherlock Holmes, and he also contacted some of the members of the Baker Street Irregulars, a private invitation-only club formed in 1934 and named after Sherlock Holmes street urchins, who in Conan Doyle's novels served as valuable ears-on-the-ground.

Green revealed to all he contacted, that he held the proof that this auction should not be allowed to go ahead, for he had a copy of Dame Jean's Last Will and Testimony, he said, in which she bequeathed her late father's papers, diaries and books to the British Library. This was the most damning evidence; these items should never have turned up at Christie's auction house, Green believed, and with the amassed assistance of his fellow Sherlock Holmes experts and scholars, Green approached the Houses of Parliament to present his proof. It was around this time that Green first began to notice that his actions may have attracted the wrong kind of attention. He telephoned a reporter at the London Times and told him, "Something might happen to me." However, he didn't elaborate any further than that. He told his sister Priscilla that "Someone" was after him. Later, speaking for the first time since Green's inquest, his sister Priscilla West told David Smith of The Guardian that when she arrived in haste at her brother's West London home, increasingly fearful for his welfare, she got no reply when she rang his doorbell repeatedly. She summoned the police, who broke the door down. They found Green dead in his bedroom, garrotted by a shoelace. The wooden kitchen spoon was still entangled in the lace. Prior to the official inquest, Westminster Coroner Dr. P. Knapman asked Holmes afficionados if they could find any incident in the canon of Sherlock Holmes stories which Green may have been seeking to re-enact. The coroner was told that there was only a single 'garrotter,' who was an agent of the Victorian sleuth's arch enemy Professor Moriarty. The Coroner concluded that garrotting was 'a painful way to kill oneself, and very unusual.'

Green's sister told The Guardian that she had spoken to her brother, "Several times during the week before he died. He was clearly very stressed about these papers. He became delusional. He said he felt the world was "Kafkaesque" – certain people were doing what he wouldn't expect, certain people were not doing what he'd expect and so on. He said he hadn't slept for several nights. At one point he said he wasn't sure I was me. I was very concerned about his state of mind that I went to see him. Richard was very disturbed but I wouldn't have said suicidal. I have one or two recent files from his computer and they are models of lucid argument. He was afraid of something. It was nebulous." Nicholas Utechin, editor of The Sherlock Holmes Journal, told Smith of The Guardian that he had known Green for 40 years. "I have no doubt it was suicide due to his mind being deranged. I spoke to him by phone for half an hour before his death. He seemed to be accusing me of conniving and conspiring. He thought people were out to get him and he was being bugged. I do not for one-minute think there was anything in the suggestion of bugging or being followed."

Smith says, 'Among the wilder theories is that Green feared he was being spied on by the Pentagon. One friend, who wished to remain nameless, said Green had become paranoid about Jon Lellenberg, a strategy analyst in the office of US Defence Secretary Donald Rumsfeld.' Lellenberg, like Green, was also a highly respected scholar of Sherlock Holmes too and a leading figure in The Baker Street Irregulars. In fact, Lellenberg had contributed to Christie's catalogue for the upcoming auction, and he had been in London 'in the week of Lancelyn Green's most erratic behaviour.'

Lellenberg however told the reporter, "I have no knowledge of why he was paranoid. It would be silly and delusional to be concerned about me because the work I do has nothing to do with intelligence and surveillance at any level.' He said he hadn't seen Green in over a year, when Green travelled to the US to give a Holmes lecture. Lellenberg spoke highly of Green's research and scholarship, and he said there had been no falling out with Green before his death.

Green's older brother, Scirard Lancelyn Green, was not so sure that this was a clear case of suicide however. He told Smith, "There's no note. He was very organised and tidy. I can't believe he would have done something without leaving some kind of evidence." Close friend Owen Dudley Edwards also said, "I don't think my friend committed suicide. He was absolutely devoted to his mother and he would have done anything rather than put her through the incredible grief she has been caused. Not all the circumstances of the death are consistent. He had finished a dinner with wine, yet when found dead there was a bottle of gin with him. You don't combine the two and he wouldn't have done so. The balance of probability is in favour of him being murdered. It's possible somebody who had something to fear decided he was better off out the way."

Green lived alone at the time of his death and was single. Although his last relationship had ended some years ago, he maintained a close friendship with his former boyfriend, Lawrence Keen, who worked as a carer for the elderly. On the night Green died, they had gone out for dinner. As they were walking back to Green's apartment, Keen later said that Green pointed to a car they'd just passed and said the car was following him. He added that "Someone was after him." Green said the person was "An American." When they went inside Green's apartment, Keen said Green told him they must talk outside as "His whole apartment was bugged." Mr. Keen told the inquest, "His mind was not its normal self and he was telling me someone in America was trying to hunt him down in the Sherlock Holmes Society."

At Green's inquest, his general practitioner supplied Green's medical notes, and it became clear that there was no indication Green had ever suffered from or been treated for mental illness. Those who knew Green said he was level-headed, organised, and a sensible, practical man. When Green had been found dead, nothing appeared to have been stolen from his apartment, although possibly it would have been difficult for the police to know immediately if anything from his huge collection had gone. On the night of Green's death, his sister Priscilla had tried calling him. She got no answer from Green and her calls went straight to his landline anasphone. To her surprise, an American man's voice requested her to leave a message. Had an American man been inside Green's apartment on the night of his murder? Well, it would later transpire that Green had wiped his own voice message from the ansaphone and in its place was this American voice. The police managed to deduce that the American voice was actually pre-programmed into the machine upon purchase. Some of his close friends however wondered; had Green erased his own voice message so that the American voice would be heard; as a clue about who might be after him? Had Green been trying to help people solve his impending murder? Or, had someone else been in his apartment and wiped his voice message? But if so, why would they do that? Was his murderer trying to shift the blame onto someone else? It's said that the police did not check for any fingerprints in Green's home.

The coroner Dr Paul Knapman was quite flummoxed about what happened to Green that night. He had once attended a meeting of the Sherlock Holmes Society to conduct a mock inquest into the murder of a character in one of the Sherlock Holmes stories, in which a corpse is discovered in a locked room. He couldn't solve it. At Green's apartment, there had been no sign of a forced entry, and no evidence anyone else had been inside the apartment that night. However, both the pathologist Sir Colin Berry and the coroner Dr Knapman felt that the manner of Green's death was not one a person would choose to carry out upon themselves; for it would have been very difficult. The problem was they said, that invariably one would pass out whilst garrotting oneself, and therefore be unsuccessful in completing the garrotting. In fact, the pathologist stated that he had only seen one similar death in all his 30 years of practise. The Coroner said, "To put a lace, which must hurt, around the neck and continue to twist it. It's an unusual form of death, that can be done by others." Green left no suicide note, and for an avid writer and collector of notes, journals and letters, most people, including the coroner, found this highly unusual. The Coroner declared the cause of Green's death to be 'An open verdict.'

Could Green have been tricked into opening the door for a delivery man, who turned out not to be delivering? Many of his friends were insistent that while Green was a connoisseur of wine, he would never have bought a bottle of gin; yet there on his bed beside him lay a bottle. Had someone forced him to drink the gin, then garrotted him? Had Green opened the door to someone he trusted, who had brought with him a gift of gin? Yet isn't garrotting more the art of a professional assassin, rather than a literary rival of Conan Doyle's works? It's an unusual method of killing, and one that harks back to centuries gone by, but perhaps that was the idea. Had a wealthy private collector objected to Green's unrelenting attempt to stop the auction and hired a "hit-man" to do away with Green's meddling, with the added flare of a rare and dramatic style of murder? Or was it someone intent on making it a murder befitting a scene in a Sherlock Holmes story? Had Green done this himself? Had he tried to frame a literary rival, an arch enemy as fearsome as Sherlock Holme's Moriarty, for his murder? Although would he really have gone to the extent of killing himself to do this?

Or did Green feel that his eternal quest for the lost papers had all been for nothing; that his opus would never be completed now, and he killed himself in a fit of despair? Did he stage his own elaborate death as befitting for a central role in one of Holmes' stories? Did Lancelyn-Green deliberately attempt to leave an unsolvable murder-mystery that would intrigue, perplex and puzzle all afficionados of Sherlock Holmes for years to come?

Perhaps the most intriguing aspect of the manner of Green's death is that he was known by everyone for only ever wearing slip-on shoes. So where did the shoe-lace that garrotted him come from?

Was Richard Lancelyn Green killed by a rival, an assassin, or by his own hands?

Chapter Two:

The case of Pauline Picard

Sent by special cable from France on May the 27th 1922, The New York Times reported on a very curious case. 'A baffling mystery is exciting the inhabitants of the small Brittany village of Goas Al Ludu in the Brest district. Early in April, a little girl, Pauline Picard, disappeared from her parent's farm, all searches proving fruitless. However, just as her parents had given up all hope of ever finding their daughter, it was reported from the far-away town of Cherbourg, that a small girl had been found there, whose age and appearance corresponded very similarly to that of the missing Pauline.'

Her parents hurried to Cherbourg to be reunited with her, and on meeting the child they said with much relief that this child was indeed their lost 2-year-old daughter, Pauline. Strangely however, it was reported that the child did not seem to recognise her parents at all, and she remained completely mute; unable or unwilling to speak when addressed in the Breton dialect she had grown up speaking. Her parents and the nuns at the orphanage in which she had been placed, put this down to the trauma of what she had been through. Somehow, she had ended up over 200 miles from her home. The nuns had received the little girl after she had been found wandering alone among the shops in the town centre. Mr. and Mrs. Picard joyously took their daughter back home to be with her eight siblings on the family farm. Immediately upon their return, her brothers and sisters were overjoyed to see the little girl returned unharmed and they embraced her back into the fold. 'The child was recognized by neighbours, and the police officer who accompanied her from Cherbourg was satisfied that she really was Pauline Picard,' reported the French Newspapers. As for her unexpected vanishing, she had disappeared from the family farm one afternoon while out playing in the yard. As soon as her absence was noticed, her family and neighbours had searched the farm and the surrounding land, and summoned the police to assist them. No sign of Pauline could be found. The search for her continued for days, then weeks; every patch of land thoroughly searched, but they found no clues about where the child could be. Le Matin said, 'The gendarmes and police inspectors spent the next month searching the country but found no trace of the child. People began to think that little Pauline had been eaten by a wild boar,' while The New York Times said, 'It was thought she must have been carried off by gipsies, although none had been observed in the neighbourhood at the time of her disappearance.' But now she was home safe; or was she? On Saturday May the 27th 1922, The Pall Mall Gazette reported, 'A strange mystery which revives another mystery is engaging the attention of all of Brittany. A mystery of a lost, a found, and a dead girl.' What did they mean? Says Le Matin, 'The adventure appeared to have reached a happy ending until yesterday a startling discovery was made which makes the whole affair more mysterious than ever. A farmer crossing a field about a mile from Goas Al Ludu discovered the horribly mutilated body of a small girl, entirely naked and the head cut off. Close by, carefully folded, lay the clothes.' The Pall Mall Gazette said, 'Her body was in the last stage of decomposition.'

After the farmer stumbled across the terrible scene of the headless, mutilated little body, he hurried back to the village to summon the gendarmerie, and they went to the spot at which the small body lay. Many curious villagers followed them, including Mr. and Mrs. Picard. The Picard's immediately recognised the neatly piled clothes as those which their daughter Pauline had been wearing on the day she vanished. But how could this be?

Three days later, a further report came. 'Closer investigation of the circumstances under which the body was found and the medical examination have added still further to the detectives' difficulties. So careful was the search made at the time of Pauline's disappearance that the body would have been discovered had it been lying where it was found,' and, 'The body could not be identified, the face having been partly devoured by foxes.' Was this Pauline after all? But if so, why had they not found her body in all the searches? Or, was it a different little girl? The Picard's said Pauline had been safely returned to them; but why were Pauline's clothes now lying beside another small body that no longer had a face? If it were Pauline, how could her parents and siblings and neighbours mistake her for another child? If the body found was Pauline's, then who was this little girl now living with the Picard's?

'The Picard's are now uncertain whether the child they have been nursing for more than a month is really their own,' said the French newspapers. And as for the police, 'They are now faced with a three-fold task - to discover the murderer, identify the murdered child, and, if she is proved to be Pauline Picard, discover the identity of the little girl from Cherbourg.'

However, there is yet another twist. 'The most startling discovery of all is that the unrecognizable head found close to the child's body is not the skull of a small child but of a grown man.' So, there were now two dead people. The body of a child and the head of a man. So, we have a missing girl, a girl returned who is a doppelganger of Pauline, a dead girl, and a dead man; all of whom remain unidentified! Which out of these is Pauline? Who is the girl fetched from Cherbourg? Who is the child's body in the field? And where is her head? Where is the dead man's body, and who is he?

The Nottingham Journal of Tuesday the 30th of May 1922 wrote, 'A telegram from Bretton states that the post-mortem held on little Pauline Picard shows that the 3-year-old child who was lost died of hunger.' They seem to be accepting that the body is Pauline's, yet surely, she didn't die of hunger; she died because her head had been cut off?

Or does it mean that her head was cut off after she was dead? The next day, The Yorkshire Post reported, 'To the astonishment of the inhabitants of the village: the conclusion is that the child died as a result of an accident. The state of the remains did not permit examination to throw light on the manner of death, but the fact that the head was severed from the body and the clothes were folded by the side of the remains had led to the conclusion that a crime had been committed,' and, they added, 'The terrible mutilations according to the authorities, might have been caused by the foxes, which might, it is stated, have shaken off the clothing. Those who do not attribute the child's death to accident think that in this case the clothes would not be clean and carefully placed together.' After all, foxes can't fold clothing.

If it was Pauline, her body and clothes did not seem to have been lying there for long. The prolific Fortean writer of the day, Charles Fort, born 1874, wrote 'It could not long have been lying, so conspicuous, but unseen. The body placed in a conspicuous position, as if planning to have it found? It seems that the clothes, also conspicuous, had not been lying there for several weeks, subject to the disturbing effects of rains and wind.' Someone had killed and decapitated a little girl, hidden her away somewhere, then taken her to the field and placed her clothes neatly beside her, along with a man's skull, it would seem. Did the man's skull belong to the little girl's murderer? But then where was his body? Or had they both been killed by someone else?

Villagers talked among themselves and to the authorities. 'People are talking about two strangers who were seen in the area at the beginning of April,' reported le Matin. A few days later, 'A neighbour says she saw two strangers in town who hung around the farm during the time the disappearance took place,' and, that they were "watching" Pauline.' Other villagers suggested a chimney sweep came into town and enticed Pauline with candy then abducted her. But the police could not find these men. Then there was talk of a Mr. Keramon, an umbrella salesman. He had worked as a farmhand on Mr. and Mrs. Picard's farm, and the French newspapers say he had been invited to have breakfast with the family on the day Pauline disappeared.

As the investigation progressed, further gruesome details emerged. 'The hands and feet of the decapitated little body in the field are missing.' Meanwhile, the gendarmerie found the umbrella salesman and questioned him. They retraced his steps on the day of Pauline's disappearance, but it transpired that his travel movements on that day placed him elsewhere when Pauline vanished, and so he could not have been the person who abducted her. Next to fall under suspicion was a farmer, Mr Yves Martin, who lived close-by. He was said to have paid a visit to the Picard farm after Pauline was brought back home, and his behaviour was odd to say the least. It was reported that he was silent at first when he entered the Picard's farmhouse. He inquired if Pauline really had returned home? On hearing that she had indeed, he apparently then became quite hysterical, burst into laughter that made him sound unhinged, and with a crazy look in his eyes he muttered, "May God forgive me." What had he done? The following day he was taken to a lunatic asylum, raving mad, and there he was to remain.

Meanwhile, the Picard's finally accepted that although their little girl had now begun to speak the odd word in Breton, she was probably not their daughter after all, and they agreed to hand her back to the authorities to be returned to the orphanage in Cherbourg. The grand mystery however was far from solved. The two mystery men "watching" Pauline were never located, nor the chimney sweep, and though the umbrella salesman and the farmer now held in a lunatic asylum were both ruled out as suspects, the gendarmerie failed to come up with any other persons of interest.

Was the little body found in the field Pauline Picard? Where was her head? Who did the man's skull belong to? And where was his body? Was he Pauline's killer? Or was he killed by whoever killed Pauline? Who could have killed them and why?

Chapter Three:

Neo Babson Maximus

Neo Babson Maximus was a world-class player at a first-person shooter computer game called 'Half-Life.' On October the 11th 2007, Neo answered a phone call from his sister in which she asked him why he had deleted his Facebook profile. He told her he had not deleted it. However, it was now gone. In the same phone call, Neo told his sister cryptically, "The answer is in the periodic table." Then he vanished. When Neo had answered her phone call, he'd been fleeing through the woods. Neo Babson Maximus was running for his life; but why? And where is he now?

Neo had once been one of the top gamers in the world and he'd changed his name from Charles Allen Jnr, in part to reflect his online persona. The computer game 'Half Life' at which he was number one for some time, revolves around a central character who is a scientist who must fight his way out of a secret underground research facility where R&D experiments into teleportation technology have gone disastrously wrong. Neo was also a highly talented tennis player, who his friends said wanted to go on to play professionally. He was a University of Massachusetts Dartmouth senior, where he was studying psychology. When Neo's sister had called him to ask him about his Facebook profile, he replied that he had not deleted it and he began to become agitated, frightened, frantic. He told his sister that people were after him and he wasn't safe. His sister couldn't understand why he would be saying this. He told her she must immediately get home to their parents, because she too was not safe and that only their father could protect her. He told her he had sent emails to "important people," and that now these people were after him. He told her to "Look under the periodic table of elements for the answers." Then he hung up. When his sister tried to call him back, he did not answer. That was the last time she spoke to him. Around the same time, Neo phoned his parents and left what his father said were "Strange messages" on their voicemails. His father said it sounded like he was running at the time. Then his phone was turned off.

When enquiries were made at Neo's University, his friends said he'd been having a routine day at college before he made those calls. What none of them knew was that Neo had to take medication for bi-polar disorder. However, he had decided to stop taking his medication a while ago, believing he no longer needed it. Despite this however, no-one saw any changes in his behaviour in the days leading up to his frantic phone conversations, apart from one minor thing. His friend Mason said that after playing a game of tennis together that day, Neo had helped himself to Mason's food as they sat eating in the college cafeteria, although perhaps Neo had just been joking around. In fact, his friends were very shocked when they learned he had bi-polar disorder, because they would never have guessed from all their interactions with him. Neo's parents also said that while he had appeared uptight at times recently, they had seen no worrying signs. They added that he had never suffered a breakdown in the past. Had Neo now tragically experienced a psychotic episode? That would surely be the most logical thing to think at face value, and yet, would it not be a very strange coincidence that he believed "important people" were after him because he was suffering delusions or paranoia, and then he did disappear? - That he feared he was being hunted down and would be taken, and then he was taken, by some other cause, for some other reason? Or, was it simply all in his mind? And yet, if so, where was he?

According to his friends, Neo had spent a normal day at college and played a game of tennis. He'd arranged to meet a friend later that evening in the college car park to go to a party. He never showed up. The following night, he broke into a woman's home a couple of miles away and entered her bedroom, believing for some reason that it was the home of his friend, Mason. When the woman whose home he'd broken into woke up, he apologized politely and then jumped out of the second-floor window, then ran off into the woods.

In his phone messages to his parents the day before, he'd told his father he was heading to Texas, while he told his mother he was thinking of going to Florida. His parents had thought perhaps he was joking with them, or had planned to head out of town for a couple of days with his friends, and they weren't overly concerned. Was Neo suffering from a manic episode and running on adrenaline and heading off somewhere on an adventure? Or, was he trying to throw his pursuers off by leaving false clues about where he was going? When Neo's parents tried to reach him, their calls all went unanswered, and so they decided to contact college security and then the police. Neo's off-campus apartment was searched, but he was not there. On campus, his 1999 Ford Expedition vehicle was found parked in the college parking area. The police said it looked like he'd been sleeping in his car, and his friends said this was something he sometimes did. Police checked his computer to see if they could find any information that might help them ascertain where he was, but his computer had been wiped. Everything was gone. All documents, all emails. His sister and his parents did not believe for a second that Neo would have done this himself voluntarily. Any evidence of him sending emails to "important people" was now gone too. Who were these people? And why would they be after him? Or had Neo become confused and no such emails existed? He was highly intelligent. Was it possible he had hacked into something he shouldn't have? And yet Neo had never shown any criminal proclivities in the past. Ever since his disappearance in 2007, his family, friends and online sleuths have tried to figure out what happened to Neo and solve the riddle of his vanishing. His family hired private detectives, but this was to no avail. What did Neo mean in the only clue he left behind? "Look for the answers in the periodic table?"

It seemed to be all there was to go on. The words 'Half Life' can be formed from some of the elements in the periodic table. Hydrogen is H. Al is aluminium, Li is Lithium, F is Fluorine, and so on, although surely any number of words can be spelled from the elements listed in the table? Or did his disappearance have something to do with his online gaming? Had an argument broken out between players? Was a jealous rival threatening him? And yet Neo no longer played that game like he used to in the past. And why would other gamers be "important people"? Had a person or persons used the game as a means to make make contact with him? Persons who had ill intent toward Neo? Had they lured him, abducted him? Although what possible reason could there be for doing such a thing?

Could it be that Neo was referring to the Periodic Table itself, as a whole? Alchemists created the Periodic Table. Alchemists are often described as the first Chemists. They developed an extraordinary language, rather than the chemical symbols we use today, to describe all manner of things, from chemical reactions to philosophical tenets, and Alchemy at its most fundamental is a principle or belief. It can be the main principles of a religion or a philosophy. Alchemy is a credo, a dogma. Alchemy in its purest sense is a search for transcendence of the soul through 'illumination,' a search for eternal life. Alchemy encompassed physics, medicine, astrology, mysticism and spiritualism. The aims of the Alchemists were to find the Stone of Knowledge; The Philosopher's Stone, not in a literal search, but symbolically. They were in search of the elixir of immortality, of Perfected Man as a divine living god, and this encompassed arcane alchemical rites, rituals, and even sacrifice, going back centuries. For the alchemist, it represented the perfection of all matter on any level, including that of the mind, spirit, and soul. Rituals could include a drowning ritual, for representation of the dissolution of matter and identity, and the first stage of the Great ritual is The Purification, and the alchemist will later bathe in a tincture taken from the dead man, it is said. Could this have anything to do with Neo's disappearance? Or is that simply fantastical? Maybe Neo simply meant look physically under the book of periodic table in his room? Maybe he had hidden something there?

On October the 18th, one week after his disappearance, a pair of sneakers were found along Chase Road near the woods Neo had been fleeing through. They were confirmed to be Neo's. His backpack was also found in the backyard of a house on Slocum Road, also near the woods. A three-day search had been carried out, using dogs, ATV's and helicopters. A four-square-mile radius was intensely covered, through woods and marshland. Lieutenant Ken Cotta, the public information officer for Dartmouth police department said police had conducted reverse 911 phone calls in the areas around which Neo had disappeared, asking people if they had seen any signs of Neo. He said that three searches with police dogs and a blood hound, in the area Neo had been running, found nothing. One year later on a Saturday morning, a huge group of volunteers including many Dartmouth Mass students gathered to search again. They did a 'line search' across four square miles of fields and woods around the University. Meanwhile, professional search and rescue groups arrived from far-afield to assist in the efforts. Members of the American Red Cross came, and four private investigation firms. Private Investigator John W. Leccese told South Coast Today news that no clues had been found. He said there had once been a possible sighting of Neo getting into a truck near the intersection of Route 6 and Cross road, but that enquiries carried out with truckers' unions had resulted in no further information coming forward. He said the lack of leads was disturbing to him, especially when no clues had been found in the searches either. Dave Polmon of the Connecticut Canine Search and Rescue told South Coast, "On a windy day a dog can pick up the scent of a person from 200 yards," and he added that a properly trained dog can even pick up the scent of a body underwater. After Neo disappeared, The Standard Times covered the first searches. By October the 27th, police had decided to suspend the ground search because of lack of evidence. 'Efforts to find Mr. Maximus broadened to include searches of area homeless shelters and hostels, police said, but so far, officers' visits to a number of these sites have proved fruitless. Media reports did net a few calls from people who reported seeing someone matching Mr. Maximums description near the Dartmouth Mall and Walmart, but the leads turned up nothing, police said.'

A witness claimed to have seen Neo running shoeless and shirtless. A trucker also came forward to say he believed he had seen a shirtless and shoeless man who looked like Neo talking to a truck driver and trying to hitch a ride. "Where do we go from here?" said Private Investigator Leccese. Neo Babson Maximus is still missing. Did Neo have a tragic breakdown? Where could he have gone? Were people really after him? And what did he mean that the answer lies in the Periodic Table?

Chapter Four:

Mr. Rouse & Mr. Popper

In November 1930, in the Swan and Pyramid Public House in North London, a conversation was taking place between two men. If anyone else in the pub had caught any part of the conversation taking place between the two men standing at the bar, they would have noticed nothing strange or unusual. They might have noticed that one was drinking beer and the other lemonade, and one of the men was more smartly dressed than the other, but there was nothing else of note that would have drawn their attention.

It would later transpire that the two gentlemen had met outside the public house, and one had invited the other one inside. It was November the 5th, although one of them would later say it was the 2nd or 3rd. Later, one of the men would say that the other man with him was "Approximately forty years of age, between 5 ft 6 and 5 ft 8 inches tall, had a slight brogue, and had a boxing or sports tattoo on his right forearm." He would say that the man had been wearing police boots, which the other man explained had been given to him by the London police. He was also carrying a sports diary.

The following day, at approximately 1:50 a.m., November the 6th, two young men were making their way home along a country lane after attending a Guy Fawkes Night dance in the town of Northampton. They were heading to their homes in the nearby village of Hardingstone, when their attention was drawn to a fire ahead of them. Their first thought was that this was a bonfire, because of course it was Fireworks Night, but it was a fierce-looking fire. As they got closer, a smartly-dressed man appeared in the lane, coming toward them. As he approached them, they noticed that he was carrying an attaché case. As he reached level with them, one of the young men made a remark to the man about the intensity of the blaze up ahead, to which the man replied that somebody was having a bonfire, and continued on his way. As the two young men reached the end of the lane, they saw that the bonfire was actually a car on fire. The flames were too big for them to even attempt to put the fire out by themselves and they rushed off to fetch the village police constables. Returning as a group, the men used water from the nearby lake to put out the fire.

Horror struck them all once the flames had died out. Inside the car in the passenger seat was a charred body. Near the car, a mallet was lying in the road, with hair attached to it. Although the fire had destroyed most of the car, the license plate remained almost undamaged, and so the police were quickly able to discover the name of the owner of the car.

Strange Tales of Mystery Unexplained

The car was registered to an address in London and a few hours later, the London police visited the car owner's address. His name was Albert Rouse and he had a wife. She said he had left home early in the evening of November the 5th to drive up North for a business meeting. He had then returned at some point in the early hours of the following morning, she said, but she did not know where he was now. This was a bit strange, the police thought. They asked if she would be willing to accompany them to the police station where some of the items retrieved from the car now were. When they showed her a wallet, she identified it as her husband's, and the scraps of material taken from the clothing of the burnt man in the car also looked like her husband's clothes, she said.

At the same time as this was happening, in a house in Glamorganshire, Wales, a woman opened her morning newspaper to find her fiancé's burnt-out car pictured in a news item. Quickly she showed her fiancé, who was sitting having breakfast with her. He told her, "That's not my car." But she knew from the license plate number that it was. The Newspaper story was asking if the owner of the car had died in an accident, or if he had been murdered. Meanwhile, her fiancé quickly left the breakfast table, telling her he was going to the coach station where he would be catching a coach to Hammersmith, London. When she asked why he was not driving, he told her his car had been stolen.

When he arrived later that day at Hammersmith coach station in London, the Scotland Yard police were there to meet him. His fiancée, Phyllis Jenkins had reported him to the police after he'd left her breakfast table in Wales. While Scotland Yard awaited the arrival of the police from Northamptonshire, the man told the London police that the person in his car had been a hitcher he had picked up, and that the hitcher had set the car on fire accidentally by lighting a cigarette as Rouse fetched a can of petrol from the boot of the car. Rouse said they had run out of petrol and while he had gone to relieve himself, he left the hitcher to fill the tank up with petrol. Then the car went up in flames, he said. He said he could not rescue the man, as the car was already ablaze and the man was trapped inside. Mrs. Rouse in London had no idea Mr. Rouse had a secret fiancée in Wales.

The Northampton police arrived and they did not believe Rouse' story, namely because they'd found the mallet beside the car with hair stuck on it. It looked very much like murder to them, and they arrested him.

At his subsequent trial for murder, not one but three mistresses gave evidence about his unorthodox lifestyle, and it became clear that Rouse, a travelling salesman, did not live his life by telling the truth. An insurance inspector revealed that the feeding pipe for the petrol had been purposely loosened, presumably in order for the petrol to spill more easily and help the fire take hold. "Several" children were due imminently to be born by his mistresses, and it would seem that Mr. Rouse had got himself into a spot of financial difficulty. What better way to avoid his responsibilities than by faking his death, he thought? He coldly and calmly explained how he had chosen a victim to play the role of himself. He had spotted a man outside the Swan and Pyramid Public House in London a few days earlier, and had invited him inside for a drink. The man had looked a little down on his luck and as they chatted over a drink, Rouse thought to himself, "He was the sort of man no one would miss." Rouse said the man had told him he had no living relatives, no family. He had no job either. This would be perfect thought Rouse. This man would make the perfect stand-in. There would be no trail to follow. Rouse' luck got even better when the stranger said he needed to head North and was looking for a ride. Rouse eagerly volunteered to take him in his car, and they arranged it for a couple of days' time. On the appointed day, Rouse returned to the Pub to meet the man and they soon set off in Rouse' car. He even generously bought a bottle of whisky for the man to enjoy as they drove. By the time they reached Northamptonshire, a couple of hours north of London, the stranger had fallen asleep in the passenger seat, having drunk quite a bit of the whisky, and Rouse saw his chance. He quickly stopped the car, fetched his full can of petrol from the boot, and doused both the man and the car in petrol. Then he set the car on fire. Rouse made his way from there to one of his mistresses in Wales by hitching rides, telling the drivers that his car had been stolen.

Though he would inevitably have been caught because of the unburnt license plate on his car, many of those involved in his case remarked that Rouse' own mouth was his undoing. He simply could not stop talking. In fact, when he was arrested, the police said they found it hard to shut him up long enough for them to charge him! It was possible that this was because of a head injury he'd received during World War Two. Rouse talked so much to the police that he ended up confessing everything he had done, and why. However, the real mystery remained to be solved. Who was the man he'd set fire to? Rouse told police, "He did not tell me his name, but he did say he was looking for work, and that he was in the habit of getting lifts on lorries, but he did not tell me who he actually was. I did not care..." Rouse even admitted he had deliberately chosen Guy Fawke's night to give the man a lift up North, as he knew this would make the fire less conspicuous. Rouse was hung for his crime, but the identity of the dead man remained a puzzle.

Seventy years later in 2014, the Briggs family had been trying to complete their ancestry records by finding out what had happened to one of their predecessors, William Briggs from North London. They knew he had gone to the Doctor on the same day that Rouse had carried out his murder, and Mr. Briggs had never returned home from the Doctor's. They wondered, could he have been Rouse' victim? When William Briggs stepped out that day to go to the doctor's, he had no known enemies, or any worries in his life. His family thought he would soon come home – but when he didn't, they finally reported him missing to the police three months later. They said no real investigation was carried out by the police at the time. After a few years had passed, his sister went to the police again, looking for answers. She couldn't understand how the body in the car could not be her brother William, because the body had the same hair colour as William, she said, and he had been wearing a plum colour jacket; the same colour of jacket William Briggs had left the house wearing. The family had also discovered that William often went to the same Billiard Hall where Rouse hung out. The family asked the police to re-open the murder case, but according to the Northampton Chronicle, the police told them the records had been destroyed. Then, in 2014 the family contacted the Northampton police again, who this time put them in contact with scientists at the University of Leicester, who in turn contacted the Royal London Hospital Museum, who still held tissue samples of the victim in Rouse' car. At the time of the murder, the post-mortem had been carried out in the garage of the local Pub by a Home Office pathologist, and samples of hair had been collected. The museum agreed to release some of the samples to the University for DNA testing, along with a male DNA sample from the family of William Briggs, in order to run comparisons. After full tests were completed, it was determined however that the victim in the burnt-out car was definitely not William Briggs. What happened to Mr. Briggs remained a mystery; as did the identity of the car fire victim. Prior to this, in 2002 a pensioner living in Northampton had contacted the Chronicle Newspaper in Northampton to suggest a name. 'A name has been thrown into the ring when pensioner Daphne Townsend contacted The Chron. The retired warehouse packer believes she holds the key to the mystery which has baffled detectives for 70 years. Mrs Townsend, 74, claimed her mother in law, Elizabeth Townsend had always maintained the victim was her brother, Bill. In an exclusive interview, she told how Bill was known for his Bohemian lifestyle, travelling around the country for months, absent for much of the year. But he always returned for Christmas in the north London family's home. 1930's Christmas came and went and Mrs Townsend became convinced her brother had fallen victim to Rouse' evil plan.' The problem was, there was no proof to suggest this was Rouse' victim either.

The Chronicle says the wildest name was put forward as the possible victim in 1948. According to newspaper reports from back then, a British man called Mr. Popper had emigrated to America, where he had become involved in organised crime. Within just a few years he had risen up through the ranks to become a Lieutenant for notorious gangster Al Capone. However, it would seem that Mr. Popper then returned to England; but not before he too had faked his own death! And, in a manner identical to Mr. Rouse in England! Before Mr. Popper left America, he chose a victim; a small-time player in the gangster world who he had picked up in his Cadillac and driven to Illinois. Upon arriving in Illinois, Mr. Popper set fire to the car with his victim inside of it, just like Rouse had done. Once back in England, Mr. Popper continued his criminal ways, by escorting a man to the North of England, again eerily mirroring what Mr. Rouse had done. Mr. Popper's girlfriend later said that Popper had confided to her that his new victim "was gullible and had lots of money." Mr. Popper left London on November the 5th 1930, and told his girlfriend he would be back on Friday. He never returned. His girlfriend said she always felt that his plan had somehow backfired, and that the murderer Mr. Popper had become the murdered instead. Were the tables turned on Mr Popper? Did Mr. Rouse kill Mr. Popper in an identical way to how Mr. Popper killed his own victim in America?

The thing was, Mr. Popper did not have any boxing or sports tattoos, like the victim Mr. Rouse had picked up in the Swan and Pyramid Pub in London, if Mr. Rouse is to be believed, and he was particularly forthcoming.

So, what happened to Mr. Popper? And who was the tattooed man in Mr. Rouse' car…?

Chapter Five:

Strange Things in Warminster

Mr Arthur Shuttlewood, a reporter for the Wiltshire Times became a self-appointed chronicler for the bizarre series of events that took over a small rural community just twenty-minutes' drive from Stonehenge in Wiltshire, England. The events took place in the mid-1960's in the small garrison town of Warminster and the surrounding Cradle Hill and Cley Hill, all located beside the chalk of Salisbury plain. One winter night at 12.25 am, a local woman was driving her car when it suddenly lost power moments after she'd seen a bright orange ball ahead of her. Her attention was then drawn to the adjacent field, where she saw a "dark object" rise from the grass, after which the engine of her car started to work again.

Mr. Pell, a lorry driver, reported that as he was driving his vegetable lorry towards Warminster early in the morning of August the 10th 1965, he saw a ball of light floating approximately 50 yards in front of him, having appeared in his view from the direction of the hills beside the road. He said that it was red and it looked like a giant headlight, or, rather alarmingly, as it got closer, he said it looked like a giant eyeball! It advanced on his truck, where it proceeded to attached itself to his windscreen, he said, and there it began to vibrate against the glass. Mr. Pell's account was just one of the many strange reports catalogued by Arthur Shuttlewood.

Earlier that same morning, at around 3.45 am, a Mrs. Rachel Atwell, living just a few miles away from the road on which Mr. Pell was travelling, saw what many others in the area would also describe. She said that she was woken by a loud droning noise and got out of bed to look out of her bedroom window. She said she saw a bright light in the sky, which had "a dome-shaped top" and it appeared to be hovering over the hills opposite her house. She said that it was there for about twenty-five minutes and that it was "humming and flickering." Then it suddenly simply vanished. As for Mr. Pell in his delivery lorry, as he sat face-to-face with a single, giant eyeball vibrating against his windscreen, he was most concerned about his passengers, who happened to be his wife and young daughter. They had been sleeping in the back but had woken now, and they too were watching the giant eyeball, until it rose into the air and simply vanished! All three were understandably very frightened by this awful and incomprehensible affair. Mr. Shuttleworth himself claimed he received no less than 800 similarly strange reports from the inhabitants of Warminster. There were more sinister happenings too. Animals began to be found dead, with inexplicable instant rigor-mortis, and yet no obvious signs of trauma or injury to their bodies could be found.

The local residents became increasingly disturbed, anxious and on-edge. Many were seeing very peculiar crafts flying in the air above them; of all manner of shapes and sizes. "Here," proclaimed Shuttleworth, "is a window area to another plane of existence. There is ample evidence to support my theory," he said. "I can state with a fact that much of what happened does not include existence of astronauts from another galaxy. The pattern of events is far too complex and disturbing for this. We took photos of what we knew were typical UFO shapes and yet, when we developed our negatives, we often ended up with prints emblazoned with rows of triangles, pyramids, weird animal heads and bodies and legs, serpents and snakes, stairways and towers." These were not aliens and UFO's, he emphasised. "Many nights we heard frightening sounds which could not be identified as belonging to man or beast."

Shuttleworth had his own odd experiences. "One morning at 2.30 am, I stood at the edge of trees near Cradle Hill, mist swirling around me. The first sound came from a nearby barn. It was a heavy footstep. I walked toward the building and no one was in or around it, yet the sound was repeated several times as though someone of giant-size was walking, or rather, clumping. I tried to catch it up but the "Thing" changed direction, and I heard a shrill cackle that chilled my spine. For a few frightful seconds I was rooted to the spot, then the fear of the unknown overcame me and I fled down the trail, twisting an ankle in my rush to escape."

Local residents Neil and Sally Pike were keen UFO watchers. Neil was a bank employee, and his wife was the daughter of a former chief detective in the Wiltshire Constabulary. Neither were prone to drama, fantasy or fabrication. They were interested in the strange sights in the sky however. They often went out to the hills around Warminster to see if they could spot any flying objects in the skies above them. On August the 22nd 1972 at 10 p.m., up on Cradle Hill, Mr. and Mrs. Pike were standing by the White Gate when their attention was drawn to a hawthorn tree on the military side of the fields close-by. "From behind this tree came a sound as though some large animal – the first to come to mind was a cow – was trapped and struggling to free itself." Mr. Pike shone his torch around the tree, trying to spot it, yet he could see no animal there and no visible movements, though the sound continued. Then all of a sudden, the sound took the form of "deliberate heavy footsteps crashing through the cornfield nearby, and coming on to the roadway."

Shuttlewood says; "At this point both Mr. and Mrs. Pike were feeling a terrible sensation of fear. Sweat poured from Mr. Pike's forehead and Mrs. Pike's whole body trembled. Someone or something was approaching them but nothing was visible. Mrs. Pike's nerve broke and she ran to the car not far away. Just before Mr. Pike followed her, he heard sounds accompanying the footsteps as though of heavy breathing. He didn't stop to hear any more and fled from the hill, convinced that something undoubtedly evil was present on the hill that night."

This was not their first experience however. One winter night the year before, Mrs. Pike was at the top of the hill keeping watch, while her husband was at a location a short distance away from her, also keeping a look-out. As the night drew on, Mrs. Pike was getting ready to call an end to the uneventful evening, when she suddenly started to feel very nervous for no known reason. Then she caught something out of the corner of her eye. Turning her head, she saw the clear outline of a figure coming toward her. The moon lit-up the figure and she could see that it had the shape of a man that looked to be at least seven feet tall, but his arms were almost of an equal length and they hung loosely at its sides. It seemed to have no neck. Its head seemed to rise straight off its shoulders. Meanwhile, Mr. Pike was standing over near an old deserted military post. As he glanced at the path leading up to the post, he suddenly saw three figures of giant height. Startled, he shone his torch toward them, and in that moment the figures seemed to disintegrate into thin air; only to re-appear instantaneously in another spot, closer to him. Alone and defenceless, surrounded by these giant figures, he fled for his life in terror.

Another sky watcher, a veteran named Bob Strong, had a similar experience when he was up on the hill. The glowing body of a "Thing" swished down over the hill and then he heard heavy footsteps thumping. Said Shuttleworth, "All these stories, no matter how bizarre, are verifiable. All the observers will attest to them, and although incredible to our way of thinking, we must keep in mind that they represent a truly alien pattern of behaviour," although of course he didn't mean they were literally alien. He believed they were something from another plane of existence.

Perturbing and ominous detonation noises were being recorded in the area too. These "detonations" rocked houses, and some residents found themselves suddenly thrown to the ground by the intensity of the sounds. A "monstrous orange flame" was reported, which according to the witness, was "crackling and hissing." A local housewife was setting off for Church at 6:30 a.m. on Christmas morning when she became very frightened by a loud crackling noise coming from the sky above her. At first, she thought it had to be a lorry spreading grit on the nearby hill, but the noise grew louder, and it came directly over her head before drifting slowly away. She described it as sounding "like branches being pulled over the gravel paths," and it was accompanied by a faint humming sound. At this time of the morning, it being mid-winter, the sky was still dark but stars lit the sky. She could see no object above her that would explain where the noise was coming from. The lady was unwilling to give her name to the Newspapers for fear of being ridiculed, but she did add that she would like to hear of anybody else who had had a similar experience, or anybody who could explain what had happened to her that morning. Her knees were "knocking all the way to Church," she said; so great was the fear she felt. The Western Daily Press headline said, "Terror Town investigates Killer Noise!" Another headline read, "Warminster gets ready for Invasion!" Arthur Shuttleworth said, "Reputable people were coming forward - the head postmaster of the town, a vicar and his three children, a hospital matron, an army major."

Celebrities like Mick Jagger and David Bowie came, fascinated to find out what was going on. Shuttlewood told the BBC back then, "I was secretly laughing at the early witnesses – I simply couldn't believe what they were telling me was true, and yet the fact that it was true was proven to me by a personal experience I had nine months later. We call it The Thing – whether individually or collectively, for want of a better name. The first to be affected were troops at the camp. They woke just as though chimneys had been wrenched off the main barracks' roof and scattered all around. The guard turned out – they saw nothing at all. This was the same day as Mrs. Bye was heading to Church on Christmas Morning. The sounds descended on her, she felt bodily contact, as if her neck was being pressed down. She was savagely jerked backwards. She couldn't fight it off. I just couldn't believe what she was telling me. Then the head postmaster heard the same sounds. Over 800 people now have seen most peculiar things." The Warminster Journal reported that pigeons were being killed in flight, dormice were being found peppered with holes, and pheasants and partridges were being found stunned in fields. Residents were so concerned that a Town Hall meeting was called, to try to get to the bottom of what was happening. Scores of witnesses shared their stories, and the mystery became known as "The Warminster Thing." It was hoped that the meeting would bring answers from the authorities; but none were forthcoming. They had no idea what was going on!

Fifty years later in 2015, reports from the Ministry of Defence were de-classified and made available at the

National Archives in Greenwich, London. Astonishingly, these archives revealed that the Ministry of Defence, the MOD, had conducted their own investigation into "The Warminster Thing." Apparently, their investigators came to the conclusion that meteors were the culprit. Meteors, not fully burnt up in Earth's atmosphere, could they said, trigger all these incidents and encounters that the residents of Warminster had reported; strange orbs, streaks of lights in the sky, cars suddenly failing to work. Meteors too were also the cause of the eerie heavy breathing and the thumping footsteps, and the giants with no necks up in the hills around Warminster, they said! Or rather, they said that these were "Psychological." The MOD report described the lights and orbs as 'Loose formations of buoyant plasma objects,' and that their behaviour was not completely understood. Atmospheric dust could also contribute to the formation of 'dusty plasmas,' which could be the cause for other strange types of sightings. They emphasized; these sightings in Warminster were 'neither hostile countries military technology nor incursions by flying objects of an intelligent extra-terrestrial or foreign origin, and represented no hostile intent.' They said that these plasma meteors were also, in their opinion, responsible for the interpretation witnesses gave to their strange sightings, because close proximity to meteor residue could affect people's brains and cause them to have incorrect recollections of what they believed they had seen! The MOD said that most of the sightings having 'unfamiliar or abnormal features,' were made by 'witnesses deemed credible' but that these witnesses were in 'unusual circumstances' and have 'misunderstood' the 'natural phenomenon they are witnessing.' But how did they know this? Did they have any proof? How could someone mistake seeing a giant with a triangular head, no neck, and arms as long as its body? I wonder if the witnesses would agree with the MOD's interpretation?

One afternoon on September the 26th 1965, Mr. Shuttleworth received a telephone call at home. The caller said his name was Kaellsen and he claimed to be from a planet called Aenstria. Shuttleworth, perhaps presuming this to be a prank call, invited the man to come to his house. In what felt like just seconds, Shuttleworth heard his doorbell rang. This of course was decades before mobile phones had been invented, yet Kaellsen was on the doorstep already. He had, according to Shuttleworth, "a high and long forehead, not particularly wide. Two startling tufts of pure white hair were brushed back to either side from the front. His eyes were bright, set wide in a long and narrow face. I noticed no trace of pupils at their centre, yet cannot be positive he had none. If he had, they were indiscernible. Slender, pointed fingers of his hands were meeting in a repeated movement in front of him as he stood there, immobile. His lips were a bluish tinge. On each cheekbone, high up, were similar blue blotches or contusions. Before speaking, he drew in a deep breath with a low whistling sound that puckered his lips and mouth. Then, before taking another breath, his words tumbled out in a lengthy flow of sentences." He warned of a coming "apocalypse." He said he came in peace, but Shuttleworth said he felt that Kaellsen could cause great harm to him, should he wish to.

The sightings continued. In November of 1965, a retired RAF Captain and his wife were returning home to Warminster at around 1:30 a.m. when they were forced to brake suddenly. Their headlights lit up a human figure dressed in all black, wearing what looked like a balaclava or a black mask with only his nose visible. On the opposite side of the road another human figure appeared, who seemed to be staggering over a hedge. It seemed to be a young man who looked to be completely naked apart from a jacket, and who appeared to be injured in some way. As the RAF captain and his wife got out of the car to help him, the figures instantaneously vanished.

In another odd encounter, a Mr. Reginald Roberts was out driving at approximately 8 pm when he was surprised by a figure clad all in grey, "with steaming fair hair" who jumped out in front of his car. Mr. Roberts braked and got out of his car to investigate, but the figure had already vanished. A herd of cows in a field nearby disappeared. One night they were there; the next gone. The farmer searched all of the fields nearby, but found no signs of them. The following day, the cows reappeared, all huddled together in a corner of the farmer's field, appearing to be rather anxious.

Though in time, the sightings died down, the mystery of 'The Warminster Thing,' was never really solved.

Chapter Six:

The Runcorn Riddle

Another very odd series of events took place in the district of Runcorn, near Liverpool in Northern England, a few years before "The Warminster Thing." This time, it became known as "The Runcorn Thing."

At a remote, rural 15th Century farm, animals were being found dead. Specifically, pedigree pigs which were being bred by farmer Mr. Crowther and his wife. More than fifty of their pigs had been found dead, one after the other, over a number of days, and yet despite the assessment of several veterinarians, no-one could find the cause of their deaths. Each morning, the farmers would find another pig dead, or several, and yet they had no injuries, no disease; nothing that could cause them to die. How they died and why, confounded all the vets, and despite all tests being carried out, including specimens being sent away to laboratories, no answers were forthcoming. All were dumbfounded. The pigs would always appear to be fine and fit when the farmer saw them on his evening rounds before retiring to bed. Yet by the following morning, several of them would be dead.

Even more mysterious was what Mr. Crowther told the local newspaper about it. "After the last one died, I saw a large black cloud about seven feet in height. It was shapeless apart from there were two prongs poking out at the back and it was moving around in the yard. This shapeless mass approached me, stopping at about five feet from me. Then it turned in the direction of the pig sty and went in there." In the farmhouse kitchen, unbeknownst to the farmer, his wife had her own terrifying experience with an indefinable black mass. She described it as such; "It was smaller and wider. It was like smoke being drawn by suction." The declassified Ministry of Defence report into Warminster had said, "There is always the possibility that some reported events have a supernatural basis," but they had swiftly added, "Or, are due to a mental condition of a witness." The thing was, everyone locally knew the farmers Mr. and Mrs. Crowther very well, and no-one would ever have said they suffered from any kind of mental instability or were unbalanced in any way. If we are however to accept that Mr. and Mrs. Crowther could have, as the report suggested, become mentally ill and imagined this 'Thing,' surely few could argue that there still needed to be an explanation for the deaths of their pedigree pigs?

Mr. Crowther went into more detail about what he saw. He said it appeared in his kitchen "with glowing eyes and two long arms that terminated in pincers." He said that it was close enough to touch and that it felt solid as it closed in on him, then the two "pincers" reached for his throat, as if to choke him! On another occasion when it confronted him in the kitchen, the farmer rushed to turn on the light and he brushed past it accidentally, touching its rear prongs which were, he said, "like blunt sticks." As the light came on, it was gone.

At the same time as the events at the pig farm were unfolding, in the nearby village of Runcorn, at number 1. Byron Street, a household was under siege by something Life Magazine called, "Brutus," although the local newspaper and Issue 28 of the Cheshire Magazine called it 'The Runcorn Thing!' 'In Runcorn, England, Sam Jones and his family are wining distinction but losing sleep by living with a poltergeist they call "Brutus," said Life Mag. 'The Poltergeist, German for an ornery ghost, moved into their house last August. He has been living there ever since, throwing books, water pitchers, and broken furniture around the room. Two policemen, lurking in the bedroom with flashlights, once actually caught a chest on the move, and Brutus has so convinced other investigators that he now gets great publicity. Reporters and sightseers come to sip tea in the kitchen and listen while he wrecks the bedroom. There are those who suspect him because he acts up only late at night when the shades are drawn and when Sam Jones is in the room. John Bury moved into the haunted bedroom to be with John Glynn after the ghost arrived. "He's my friend, so I'll stick with him," Bury explained. Grandfather Sam Jones, widowed and retired, refuses to let the ghost dislodge him from his favourite room. Sam's sister-in-law, Lucy Crowther says, "I'll never go upstairs again," but does so in the daytime. At night, she crosses the street to sleep in a neighbour's house. John Glynn, Sam's grandson says he has lost 8 pounds since the ghost came and made him chain smoke!' As for the grandfather, 'The ghost wakes him covered by books and debris. Scars show where other missiles struck the wall.' There is a photo of a chair 'showing how legs match digs in the wall made when the ghost is there. Since the ghost works in the dark, nobody sees the missiles fly.'

Rather interestingly, it appears that Sam Jones at Byron Street knew the farmer Mr. Crowther because he had worked at the farm. But let's begin at the beginning of events at Mr. Jones' house, number 1 Byron Street, Runcorn. In August of 1956, Mr. Sam Jones, aged 68, his sister-in-law Mrs. Lucie Jones, his grandchildren John and Eileen Flynn, and a 59-year-old spinster, were all living together in the same household. At the time, they were also joined by Mrs. Jones's son and his daughter-in-law, who were visiting. Grandfather Sam shared his bedroom with his grandson, John, who was aged 17 and worked as an apprentice draughtsman. Lucy Jones and Eileen shared another bedroom. The spinster Mrs. Whittle had her own room, which was opposite the grandfather's room.

Soon, an investigator from the Society for Psychical Research in London, and a whole host of journalists would be arriving to try to get to the bottom of what was going on. It all began when the residents of the household had retired for the night. No sooner had they gone to bed when loud noises began to be heard, and they appeared to be coming from the bedroom of the grandfather and his grandson John. The noises got increasingly louder, rousing each of the occupants from the other bedrooms and causing them to inquire as to the commotion. Between them all, no answers were forthcoming; no-one could account for the thuds and bangs, and with the noises continuing they had no choice but to return to bed, perplexed but attempting to get some sleep. The noises got louder however, and that night not one of them got any sleep. The crashes continued all night. The next night it got worse. Loud bangs shook the foundations of the house, and what sounded like dressing table drawers being pulled sharply out and slammed back in again, echoed through the house. The grandfather and grandson left their bedroom, which seemed to be where the sounds were originating from, and then the noises ceased. When they returned to bed however, the noises returned. They watched as the dressing table rose into the air.

The chain of irregular events was to continue for a period of ten weeks, and they were happening at exactly the same time as the pig-slayings at Mr. Crowther's farm. When word of the night-terrors began to circulate, curious visitors began to arrive, all eager to investigate. The grandfather, Mr. Jones, said that he had lived in his house for more than 40 years and never had anything like this happened before. As for his grandson, the finger of suspicion quickly fell upon him. Could he be playing a trick on his grandfather and the rest of the household? It was the opinion of many 'experts' in the field of poltergeist and ghostly activities that frequently a teenage person was to blame for these occurrences; not because they were perpetrating a hoax, but the theory goes that it's something to do with teenage hormones and possible telekinesis! However, according to Phenomena Magazine, they discovered that trickery was afoot! When two reporters arrived, accompanied for some reason by the local publican, they began to hear banging coming from the grandfather Sam Jones and John's bedroom. They crept up the stairs with a torch and eased slowly closer to the bedroom door, then flung it open. To their surprise, they were greeted by the sight of the grandfather brandishing a heavy book and bashing it three times against the wall, then hurling it across the floor. It seemed the grandfather Sam Jones had been caught red-handed! When confronted by this, the grandfather reportedly quickly tried to cover himself by claiming he had found this book lying on his bed when he knew no book had been there moments before. He claimed he had grabbed the book and bashed it against the wall in anger, and thrown it to the floor in frustration. Was he telling the truth? Perhaps it's a reasonable enough explanation? After all, it must be exceedingly irritating to be constantly roused from sleep by the sound of crashing and banging within earshot and yet seeing no visible perpetrators to account for it? Perhaps we'd all want to take our frustration out on an inanimate object, particularly given that it seems the book had magically appeared out of nowhere? And after all, he couldn't grab hold of the ghost; for it was no-where to be seen! 'Clearly, this was definite evidence of skulduggery having taken place,' wrote Phenomena magazine, and while it did indeed look very incriminating, they added the question; 'Did this invalidate all the rest of what is supposed to have happened in the house? If people turn up expecting to see something and then see nothing, then it often makes poltergeist victims feel like fools or liars. They don't wish to disappoint visitors, and so produce false book-throwing's where once there were genuine ones.' Perhaps the grandfather so desperately wanted to be believed, after suffering night after night, that he needed someone, anyone, to believe him, to help put an end to his misery? There were also many more incidents which simply had not been skulduggery. A Mr. Davies, a visiting businessman, attested to having seen a cardboard box in suspension above the bed. "Its movement was not that of an ordinary trajectory, but almost as if it were being carried with directional intent." On another occasion, a jigsaw floated through the air. Items would continue to be thrown around the bedroom when several people were sitting on top of a reclining teenage John, to ensure that he was not the perpetrator of such events. At other times, John was physically lifted out of his bed by unseen hands and placed unceremoniously onto the floor.

On another occasion, even when the dressing table drawers were sealed closed, they continued to open and slam closed, or simply rattled menacingly. The mirror in the bedroom swung backwards and forwards on its pivots, as though blown by great gusts of wind, though no windows in the bedroom were open. Three large policemen were apparently thrown from the empty chest they'd been sitting on. In other rooms of the house, a grandfather clock moved of its own accord and by a distance of approximately five feet. A smaller clock shattered as if it had been hit by a mallet. The kitchen ceiling began to crack. China and crockery would be violently smashed. A policeman who had been called out to the house at the start of the events said that in his opinion, the teenage boy was in a state of "nervous collapse."

A spiritualist medium called Mr. Francis visited, and he held a séance. During this séance, two bibles were thrown across the room in front of many witnesses. The Reverend W. H. Stevens, a local Methodist minister, was hit over the head with a dictionary as he entered the house.

Witness Thomas Barrow, aged 18, who was serving in the Army at the time and was a friend of the grandson John, provided a written account of his experiences at the house on Byron Street. "John asked me to stay in the bedroom, to which I agreed. On four nights I witnessed the destruction of furniture and the police being lifted in the air and dropped down, after which they promptly departed. We asked the spirit to give his name by tapping twice through the alphabet and it tapped the name JUJU and said he was an African Witch Doctor! I noticed each night I was there that Miss Whittle, the spinster in the adjoining room, it never seemed to disturb her.'

Researcher Joseph Braddock carried out his own investigation into 'The Runcorn Thing,' only months after it happened in 1956. 'It is, as far as I know, the most well attested, and in one part the most sinister story. These odd happenings were carefully investigated by several intelligent, experienced and reliable witnesses, so that upon the evidence, I believe this case to be genuine. If at the end of my account the reader should feel only extreme bewilderment and be silently protesting "In everyday life these things cannot happen!" I would agree that the events on the farm are not easily believable."

Minister Stevens, the Methodist superintendent for the district of Widnes, who visited the house on Byron Street on a few occasions and who knew Mr. and Mrs. Crowther at the pig farm, was initially very sceptical. He told Braddock in a letter, "For about 30 years I have been a member of the S.P.R. Society for Psychical Research, have read scores of books, had sittings with mediums, seances – all in search of truth. Consequently, I knew what to expect and went to investigate in a sceptical frame of mind. I came to the conclusion that this was a genuine case. The most unexpected occurrences were those on the farm. Knowing the Crowther's and having been to the farm, I cannot doubt their story. They had been badly frightened and upset. It is impossible but true." At 1. Bryon Street, Braddock says, 'The boy complained of the shadow of a person reflected upon his bedroom wall, advancing and retreating.' Of John, he says, 'In the opinion of those who knew him, he appeared to be a normal boy, bright, pleasant and of a kindly nature, with carefree spirit. He seemed neither unbalanced nor neurotic. They began hearing what sounded like scratching in a drawer of the dressing-table. They could find no mouse, nor anything to account for this, and the scratching renewed, to be succeed on other nights by far more violent sounds, loud knockings hammered in the silence. Suspecting a practical joker, Mr. Jones reported the matter to the police but when the police could find nothing normal to account for the trouble, they officially withdrew.' Reverend Stevens said that on one occasion when he was at the house, Mr. Crowther from the pig farm, 'put his overcoat on the dressing-table, remarking, "If you don't want it, give it back to me," and in that, the coat was thrown back to him three times in succession.'

Braddock noted, 'More than thirty witnesses including a team sent by the B.B.C.,' saw inexplicable things. 'The case caused a great deal of excitement in Runcorn and crowds of people gathered outside the house. The noise of the disturbance could be heard in the street. Meanwhile at the pig farm, 'Mr. and Mrs. Crowther had shunned publicity but their story was told in the Sunday Graphic on December the 27th 1953, and the Liverpool Echo of August the 28th 1954,' said Braddock, 'So it is now part of humanity's store of uncommon knowledge. It is a story, I should imagine, without parallel – that of the deaths of all Mr. Crowther's pigs, by a supernatural agent.' The Reverend Stevens said signed statements were given by the Crowther's attesting to their experiences. 'It all began when Mrs. Crowther was making a long-distance phone call,' wrote the Reverend to Braddock. 'While waiting, she saw Mr. Crowther's deceased father standing a few yards away. He was dressed as usual, smoking a cigarette with long ash, which was characteristic of him. Mrs Crowther stared in amazement, and when her call came through, she said, "I hardly knew what I was saying, for I could still see him! Then he vanished." After this, scratching started to be heard inside the drawers of a desk in the kitchen. Then the drawers would rattle menacingly.

Stevens adds, 'They are well-respected people. They told me their story with obvious sincerity, and it was plain to see they had passed through a distressing period. Mr. Crowther was in bed for a fortnight with a breakdown. They had no knowledge or interest in Spiritualism." Braddock says, 'On August the 11th, a week before the Bryon street disturbances began, the first pig died. They attached no significance to this. Before the end of the week, several more had died. Entrails were sent away for analysis; but the cause of these mysterious deaths remained a mystery. Two days after the loss of his last pig, Mr. Crowther was astonished to see what he described as "a large black could about seven feet in height, with two prongs sticking out the back." Mr. Crowther mentioned this frightening experience to no-one, for he did not wish to be labelled mad.' He didn't even tell his wife. However, unbeknownst to him, his wife was seeing this black cloud-monster too. In a letter to Reverend Stevens, Mrs. Crowther wrote, 'I saw it in the yard. It was huge, and once in the kitchen when Mr Jones called on Armistice Sunday. I saw the thing follow Mr. Jones. It travelled like smoke.' On another occasion, Mrs. Crowther said she saw the cloud in the yard and 'it blotted out the houses in the background. As it moved along, bits of paper and dust swirled about as though they were caught up by a miniature whirlwind.'

In a convergence of growing unease and fear, farm labourer Sam Jones was soon telling the farmer Mr. Crowther about what was happening in his house at 1 Bryon Street, and 'was so stricken from lack of sleep and frayed nerves that he broke down and sobbed. He implored Mr. Crowther to come and help him.' When Mr. Crowther went to Byron Street, so too did the Reverend. Mr.

Crowther suddenly exclaimed that he could see the same black-pincered-thing now lying on the bed beside the boy, John Smith, wrote the Reverend.

Says Braddock, 'Whether the pigs saw anything or not, the fact is something frightened them. Some fought. In one sty a terrified animal was found trying to climb up the wall as if to escape. One night a cow's bellowing's were heard, unusually loud and prolonged. The animal was discovered in a state of intense fear, its eyes bulging, the hair on its back on end, its body covered with beads of sweat. No cause for alarm could be diagnosed, but from that night the cow gave no more milk.'

The last sighting of the monster was back at the farm. Mr Crowther said he watched it rise up into the sky one day, where it slowly dissipated, leaving just a ball of smoke behind it. What was 'The Runcorn Thing?' Where did it come from? And how did it kill all the pigs?

Perhaps though, this is not quite the end, because not long afterwards, Miss Whittle, the spinster at 1 Bryon Street, mysteriously died by somehow falling off the top of a hill locally known as 'Frog's Mouth.' Quite how she fell, has never been determined.

Chapter Seven:

The baffling demise of Colonel Shue

When Colonel Shue was found dead in 2003, it was a scene the first responders would never forget. He was sitting in the driving seat of his crashed car. His hands and feet were bound and he had traumatic head injuries. His shirt was ripped open and his chest was exposed. He no longer had any nipples.

The mysterious manner of his death is one that medical examiners, judges, and amateur detectives have all pondered, ever since it happened. Colonel Shue was a Doctor of psychiatry. He'd met his second wife Tracy in 1988 when they were based at Elgin Air Force Base. Five years later, Colonel Shue was reassigned to Lackland Air force Base in San Antonio, Texas, and they bought a house in nearby Boerne. "Everybody loved him. I don't think in my whole life I ever met somebody who had such passion for life and just enjoyed the simple things. People loved him. He walked into a room and he just lit it up," his wife told reporter Troy Roberts. Their friend and neighbour Nina Willard said, "He had that Midwest soft-spoken mild-manner, very laid back."

When Colonel Shue died he'd just decided to retire from the Air Force. He and Mrs Shue had found their dream home in Alabama. They'd put down a deposit and were excited for their new future. Tracy told CBS, after the Colonel's death, that on the morning of April the 16th she and the Colonel talked about the new house before he set off for work dressed in his army fatigues. It was around 5.30 am. Everything was as it usually would be. But within a few hours, he would be dead.

It would later transpire that two witnesses had seen Shue's car on the highway. They had watched as it suddenly drove into the median, causing the wheels of his car to leave the road's surface and become airborne, but Colonel Shue seemed to manage to get the car back under control and he continued driving, until shortly after when he drove into a row of trees, hitting one tree, bouncing off it, and ploughing into the tree next to it, hitting it head-on. Lieutenant Roger Anderson was one of the first responders to arrive at the scene. There was no attempt to resuscitate the colonel – he was clearly dead. It was a terrible crash, but what the Lieutenant saw inside the car shocked him far more. "The T-shirt underneath had been ripped open from the chest to the naval. There was a vertical gash in the man's chest and both his nipples had been removed. On his wrist was what appeared to be duct tape. Both wrists were taped in the same way, both dangling ends. There was also duct tape at the top of his boots." Dr. Vincent Di

Mario, the pathologist who performed the colonel's autopsy said, "The case is so bizarre." The autopsy report reveals why; Shue's shirt was still tucked in, 'Yet there is a neat cut and partial tear in the centre of the T-shirt beginning approximately 2" from above where it is tucked into the pants. There are not a lot of loose fibres at the end of this cut, which is more consistent with being cut than torn? Front of the shirt bloody from that area downwards. Buttons partially torn off the camo shirt. Beneath undershorts is a small amount of white fibre material consistent with that found in a diaper,' and 'a tab with a cartoon figure consistent with a tab from a diaper,' along with 'a gel-like material adhered to the skin, also consistent with that found inside a diaper.' The left back pocket of the pants has been cut or torn in an L-shape. 'Duct tape present about each wrist and overlaying top of the boots. About the right wrist are 1 ½ loops of duct tape with a loose end. Smeared blood on loose end. About the left wrist are three loops of duct tape, which go around the wrist. Blood found on the inner duct tape,' but, 'no sign of blood on the skin.' Most strangely, as if it was not already strange enough, the medical examiner notes, 'Loose on the skin just underneath each eye are contact lenses; the one on the left is bloody and folded.' Can contact lenses fall out in a crash? Or had Colonel Shue tried to take them out sometime earlier? Or, did someone pull them out of his eyes? Isn't it a bit strange?

The Colonel had 'Massive trauma to head. Jaw has been broken.' He had multiple head fractures. And now for another strange thing; 'Chest has moderate amount of chest hair, which in areas has been shaved off. Much of the upper portion of the right side of chest has been shaved with hair stubble present.' If stubble was present, this would indicate that it had not been shaved off at the same time his nipples had been removed, wouldn't it? It would have been the previous day at least, which would surely mean the Colonel had shaved parts of his own chest. Why would he do that?

There is 'dried blood mixed with adhered pieces of glass on back of left hand.' Presumably this is from the shattered car windscreen? There is also 'blood beneath the nails of fingers.' Had the Colonel struggled, tried to defend himself? What was happening to him before he crashed? He had two missing nipples and is bound with duct tape. Surely, he was being tortured and had escaped his captors? If the blood was dried, it couldn't have been caused during the crash, could it?

And then there is another odd thing; 'Right ear partially torn down. Left pin of ear is irregularly torn.' Why would his ears be torn down? Had they been savagely pulled? There does not seem to be any other logical answer other than that he had been abducted and horribly tortured, does there? But perhaps it is not quite that simple, as we shall discover. The pathologist describes the Colonel's missing nipples in more detail now. 'The right nipple has been cut off. Almost circular incised wound is not surrounded by abrasion or contusion.' Is there any hesitation here or was it cleanly cut? The pathologist notes a 'superficial incision,' and 'five scratch abrasions' in the area of the excised nipples. Were these practice cuts? It would take a special kind of person to cleanly slice off their nipples without any hesitation at all. Did he do this, or someone else? But there is more. 'There is an amputation of the distal portion of the 5th digit of the left hand.' Part of the little finger of his right hand has been cut off. 'Lidocaine is detected in blood.' If the Colonel was tortured, why would his torturers give him an anaesthetic to numb the pain?

The pathologist addresses the circumstances of the car crash next. The Colonel was 'witnessed to make a deliberate turn to leave highway, go up an embankment and hit a group of trees without braking.' Was he not able to hit the brake? 'There is no evidence that he at any time tried to break his car.' Interestingly, 'He had reported history of psychiatric problems.'

It was also noted, there was an 'active cell phone in car.' Why would he not have called for help? The pathologist concludes that Shue 'died as result of mass craniocerebral injuries.' Colonel Shue, he concluded, according to the evidence presented to him, killed himself deliberately. He had also cut off his own nipples, hacked off part of his little finger, and bound his own wrists and ankles. Why would he do this? And was this even possible? The Colonel's wife for one, didn't think so.

Why had the Colonel not driven straight to the police or hospital for help? Why had he not used his cell phone to call the police from his car? Was it possible he was in a desperate flight from his captors, escaping in absolute panic? Was he unable to brake because he was in a deep state of shock? And yet, just moments earlier, after hitting the median of the highway, he had managed to get his car back under control. Could his captors have let him go but threatened harm to his wife or parents, if he dared to go to the police? Or, did he believe he couldn't trust anyone? And yet, the highly experienced and renowned pathologist points out in his report, 'Information provided to the office was that he had been having some problems. He had seen some of his colleagues for depression or panic attacks.'

Sometime after Shue's autopsy, a grand jury was convened by the District Attorney. Twelve ordinary citizens determined they could find no evidence of a crime taking place. Lieutenant Anderson, who had attended the scene said, "The grand jury believed that the ruling of suicide should stand." The Colonel was depressed, suffering from high anxiety and had killed himself, according to everyone. His wife however, when talking to CBS News after this, said she believed that her husband had been abducted and tortured. "What other explanation could there be?" Mrs Shue exclaimed. Dr. Maio however disagreed. "If you had been tortured like that and you had broken free, where would you go? Either police or a hospital. But he was driving away from San Antonio and the hospitals. He passed three exists to his own town. He had a working cell phone – I mean this action is not consistent with someone fleeing an assailant." Dr. Maio believed that Mrs Shue did not want to believe that her husband did this to himself. "Her view is distorted by her love," said the Medical Examiner. Dr. Maio had also noted, 'There were no wounds identified as being consistent with a struggle,' which seems quite crucial, for surely the Colonel would have put up a fight if he had been tortured?

Mrs. Shue however was not satisfied at all with the outcome of the grand jury, and she hired Dr. Cyril Wecht, another renowned forensic pathologist. "I have never seen a case as bizarre, as a-typical as this one," he said, but he disagreed with some of the official findings. "We have no injection mark identified by the pathologist in the original autopsy, none I found. No needle or syringe found. No cutting instrument of any kind to be attributed to Colonel Shue." A swiss army knife was found in the Colonel's car, but the blades were not believed to have been sharp enough to cut off his own nipples, at least according to an Air Force forensic and psychological report that was also carried out independently. Dr. Wecht said that the amount of lidocaine found in the Colonel's system was not of a high enough quantity for him to have been able to numb himself from the pain. In other words, if he had administered it himself, it would have served no purpose, but that would also mean that it would have been ineffective for his hypothetical torturers to give to him too, wouldn't it? Although again, why would his torturers want to make his torture less painful? Could the Colonel have been self-medicating with lidocaine to numb his psychological pain, given that the pathologist Dr. Maio noted that the Colonel suffered from panic attacks and anxiety? – Although, he was prescribed medication for these conditions, and Lidocaine is not known to help psychological issues, and as a psychiatrist himself, Dr. Shue would have surely known this?

Dr. Wecht pointed out that in his opinion, "There's no evidence to show Shue cut his own chest," and that "There's an equally plausible scenario to such marks. And they're called torture." Wecht also found other curious aspects to the condition in which the Colonel was found. "His fingerprints were not found on the duct tape. And no gloves were found." Had the Colonel bound his wrists and feet, while wearing gloves; then disposed of the gloves somewhere, after wiping his own fingerprints off the duct tape? Or had someone else tied him up? "I would place my bet that this was a homicide," said Dr. Wecht.

Could someone have known the Colonel's mental difficulties and orchestrated his death to make it look like a bizarre suicide, pointing the finger of suspicion away from themselves? There is more to this story, and it just gets stranger. Mrs. Shue said that her husband had for some time been receiving anonymous letters. "You may be in danger," one typewritten note said. This note was just one of many her husband received, said Mrs. Shue. "It was an anonymous letter that said essentially that a person overhead a conversation between Nancy Shue, the Colonel's first wife, and Donald Timpson, her current husband. And they were plotting to have him murdered for the insurance money." The warning note reads, 'A friend of mine told me some scary things. I don't know Don or your ex-wife. My friend told me they wish you were dead so they could collect the life insurance. I don't understand why they would have life insurance on you, but that's what my friend told me. My friend thinks they may actually be planning something. Please be careful. I had to write. If I didn't, I couldn't bear the thought of something bad happening to you that I could have prevented by telling you what I heard.'

Nancy's current husband was an active duty Air Force pilot. Nancy Shue had a life insurance policy from the time she had been married to Shue. Although they were now divorced, Nancy would still receive an insurance pay out if Colonel Shue were to die. Mrs Shue said the Colonel had asked many times for Nancy to cancel the insurance policy, but she apparently refused to do so. Mrs Shue said that after the Colonel received the warning letter, he wrote to his ex-wife Nancy, confronting her about it and telling her again to "drop the life insurance coverage on me," adding, "I feel helpless to prevent my eventual murder if you hire good assassins." Nancy's response to the Colonel's accusations that she was trying to kill him, was that she was not responsible for his letter. His former wife told him, "This may have been someone's terribly sick idea of a game or a joke." Shue's ex-wife and her husband said they were in Florida and could prove it. Could they have asked someone else to attack the Colonel? Mrs. Shue came up with an alternate theory, which she offered to CBS. 'Nancy was a board-certified sex therapist, who had,' (among other things) 'studied the practise of Sadomasochism. "I believe the injuries he sustained are consistent with an act of sadism. And they are certainly sexual in nature,"' she said. Nancy would have studied all manner of topics for her sex therapy, and because she studied Sadomasochism, it didn't mean she would actually put it into practice too though!

The other letters the Colonel received, they were threats, at least that's what he said. It's possible to get a deeper insight into the life and death of Colonel Shue by reading the forensic and psychological autopsy carried out in May

2005 by Lakeland Detachment of the Air Force Office of Special Investigation, the AFOSI. This involved 'The opinions of two board certified forensic psychiatrists, interviews, information sources and our experience.' Colonel Shue was a staff Psychiatrist at Wilford Hall Medical Centre. They interviewed his colleagues including the Chief of Psychiatry at the Medical Centre and a Staff psychiatrist, a former supervisor of the Colonel, as well as his father, wife and friends. 'It was reported that Shue had left for work at about 5.30 a.m., and this was 1 hour earlier than usual. There was no evidence of where he was between 5.30 a.m. to 8 a.m., but he was not seen at work in that time.' Where was he? Has it ever been established? Could have been abducted during that window of time? Was he meeting someone? Or was it just that no-one else was at work at that time? Military personnel are usually early risers, aren't they? And surely, he would have been observed entering through the security gates at the base?

The report continues, 'Neither part of his finger nor the excised tissue from his nipples was ever located.' If Colonel Shue's hands and feet were bound, how could he have done this to himself somewhere else, disposed of the excised nipples and finger, then driven off? Or did he tie himself up afterwards? The Medical Examiner Dr. Maio believed Shue tied himself up. Where could he have done this?

'Telephone records confirmed no calls were made from the phone in the period prior to the crash.' They point out, 'Tracy Shue, whose neighbour recovered the phone after the crash, indicated it was a clam -style cell phone and that there was blood on the inside.' Would this indicate that the Colonel had tried to use the phone to make a call? Tracy would not reclaim the car and still hasn't, because she says it's a murder and the car is a crime scene. Interestingly, the report notes there was cash in Shue's pocket 'But wallet was missing.' Inside the car was 'a straight razor and two small pocket knives, a latex glove. DNA evidence revealed presence of Shue's blood on one of the pocket knives, the glove and the steering wheel.' Yet his fingerprints weren't found. The Air Force report notes that there is 'Only one knife in crime scene photo. A swiss army type knife that was not likely to be sharp enough to create the incisions.' What was used to cut off his nipples and finger then? None of the reports state what implement Colonel Shue was supposed to have cut his own nipples and top of his little finger off with, so it is baffling to try to determine this. Curiously, 'Kendall County also reported there was an unopened package of small gauge needles in the glove box.' Why would the Colonel have needles in his car?

'The original report described Shue as making a "deliberate" turn off the highway. Dr Wecht's findings were that 'The key witnesses did not use that terminology, but merely said that the turn was sudden and that they did not see the brake lights. Wecht maintained it was possible that Shue was unable to control the car as a result of his injuries and that it could have left the road by accident. Wecht thought the duct tape with no fingerprints on it was "Suggestive of another person's involvement," and also that "The lack of any weapon that could have caused the trauma noted at the autopsy, the missing portion of his body, and the absence of his wallet all strongly and logically suggested that the trauma occurred somewhere outside his vehicle and that another person caused it.'

'A FOSI agent (for the Air Force) stated that Dr. Koonsman, the toxicologist at Bexar County Medical Examiner's office told them the test for clonazepam or venlafaxine, the two psychiatric medications Shue was prescribed, were negative.' Yet according to the Air Force, 'Clonazepam was detected in the blood in the small sample the FBI lab conducted.' So, the Colonel was either taking or not taking the meds he had been prescribed for his anxiety.

From the FOSI report we are able to learn a lot more about the Colonel's life prior to his death, and in particular it sheds light on what the Medical Examiner called his 'Psychological problems,' and why the Colonel would have been prescribed medication. Shue served as a navigator from 1970-1974. 'It appears his career was cut short at that point by medical problems.' On January the 22nd 1973, 'Shue presented to the medical clinic at Kadena Airforce Base, Okinawa, Japan.' He was stationed there at the time. 'He reported that an intruder had accosted him in his room.' In 1973, 'he had three episodes of loss of consciousness with bladder incontinence, once during a flight as a navigator,' and the forensic report comments that this could explain why he had pieces of pampers under his pants when he was found. Shue underwent extensive evaluation for a seizure disorder, but 'was determined not to have it and the etymology of these episodes was not specifically defined.' He also had 'psychiatric evaluation,' but 'no definitive psychiatric diagnosis was made, but it was thought anxiety might be playing a role.' It was some time after this that he was diagnosed as having 'Meiners disease,' a condition that can be very debilitating as it can cause severe sensations of vertigo and nausea. Perhaps the Meniere's disease was a contributing factor, if not the cause of anxiety and feelings of panic in Shue's life. It can have a major impact on a person's life and perhaps more emphasis should be given to this in understanding the Colonel's mind-set. It is a very unpleasant condition to suffer from and one in which a person can simply fall to the floor without warning, as extreme vertigo and nausea comes fast. The fear of this happening and the possibility of causing serious injury to oneself, as well as great embarrassment, could well have been the biggest cause of his anxiety and of his episodes of panic. However, there is more; Shue attended Medical school. From April 1998-2000, Shue was at the Residency with Aerospace Medicine. 'He failed to complete his required thesis.' He apparently said to the course counsellor that the University centre had a history of "pervasive cheating." The course counsellor found this strange and could not see how this would affect him completing his thesis. On another occasion, he said his laptop had been stolen and he had no back-up copy of his thesis. Again, the course councillor was surprised by this. Later, he would say his laptop had been returned, with all the data wiped. He told Richardson the counsellor, 'About threats to his life.' The Counsellor told him to tell the police. Shue replied to the counsellor with "statements that minimized the value of telling the police." Shue 'reported that on 6th December 2000 he was in the Library when he got up to use the men's room. When he returned, his laptop was gone. He reported this to school security.' This was checked by FOSI and the security report says 'His laptop was returned.' He said he found it 'Placed on the hood of his car, while parked in Boerne with a note that "if he reported anything to police, others would die."'

Shue did eventually complete his thesis and graduate. However, rather strangely, 'When he took the Aerospace Medicine Board Exam in October 2000, he scored zero points.' It was a multiple-choice test. 'No-one was able to offer an explanation for that result.' The Air Force report continues, 'He told Dr. Dionne that in 1999 he had received a letter that indicated his life was in danger due to the insurance policy his wife held on him,' and 'Anxiety progressed to the point of depression over the later part of 1999.' In December 1999, Shue was prescribed 'Fluoxetine 20 mg, and Clonazepam, for anxiety after a panic attack on base.' In 2002, he was prescribed Venlafaxine. 'Dr. Dionne quotes Shue as saying that his vigilance was "Almost paranoia," and he reported to the psychiatrist "Increased vigilance." Dr. Dionne was concerned about the possibility of paranoia when he first heard the story of the threatening letters. Shue told him he knew the story did not seem logical but that it was true. Dr Dionne noted increased anxiety in Shue's emotional expression that he thought was consistent with the story being true,' and 'Dr. Dionne described behaviours that Shue was taking to decrease his risk of being harmed. These included altering his route when driving to and from work, and using a PO Box instead of his mailbox due to the risk of it being booby-trapped.' Very strangely, 'Dr

Dionne related that about 6 months prior to his death, Shue told him he'd had a dissociative episode. Dr Dionne quoted Shue as saying that he imagined "his car went out of control on his way to work. Great violence was done (to him).'"

On the Colonel's last day, the Air Force psychiatrists discovered that his supervisor reported he'd functioned well and did not think any other staff knew that Shue was at times experiencing great anxiety. However, 'The absence of Venlafaxine in blood indicate Shue stopped the antidepressants at some point before his death.' Dr. Dionne 'Considered the possibility Shue's concerns about the threats against him arose from psychotic paranoia,' but that 'he rejected the idea because Shue's mental status was appropriate and his responses to the threats seemed logical.' However, the Air Force psychiatrists point out 'Dr Dionne did not know two pieces of information – first, he understood that Shue had informed the police about the threats' (but he had not) 'and second, Shue did not tell him that the stolen laptop had been returned with a threatening note. These two pieces of information are important because the story becomes much less credible when they are considered. If Dr. Dionne would have known, he would have had a stronger vantage point from which to challenge Shue's rationality.' Everyone wondered why had Shue not gone to the police about these letters? Were they real? Had he sent the letters?

The psychological report concluded that in their opinion, Shue had taken 'Sufficient bizarre actions' in the years prior to his death, 'that provide circumstantial support of unusual if not paranoid behaviour,' and that his death was 'Suicide,' adding, 'While he did have tape around his wrists and ankles, the tape did not look as if it had been strained against. The loops around his wrists and ankles were loose, without the pattern of stretching that would be expected if they were used to restrain him,' and 'further, the pattern in which the tape was placed on his body would be an inefficient way of binding him.' In other words, they believe the Colonel had tied himself up, binding his own wrists and ankles, after mutilating himself, and then deliberately driven into a tree.

With regards to the possibility of torturers, 'It was speculated that the lidocaine was involuntarily administered to him by an assailant as part of a drug combo intended to sedate him,' however, 'We are not familiar with its use in that role and no other sedating drugs were detected in his system.' Further, they say, 'Stopping the anti-depressant and anti-anxiety, could lead to increased anxiety. The absence of medication in his blood is a potentially self-destructive development over which no-one but Shue himself had any control. Scenarios of Shue's capture and escape are difficult to conceive.' But where was he in those missing hours? With no signs of a struggle though, how could he have escaped if he was being held? And why were his bindings so loose and unrestrained?

'If an individual/individuals had gained the complete control of Shue that would be necessary to make such precise incisions around his nipples, how would he then have escaped without further violence? Again, the absence of defensive wounds comes into play.' They did not believe it was plausible the Colonel had been abducted and tortured.

It would appear that Shue had the perfect opportunity to call for help, if he needed it, according to the Air Force. 'Shue passed a Boerne police patrol car sitting at the roadside assisting a motorist and had its rooftop lights flashing.' But was he too scared? They say, 'It is true that in the period he was observed by the witnesses, he had passed far better objects against which to crash.' In other words, if he was intent on ending his life by suicide, he could have used other, more solid objects than trees to drive into, yet he didn't. Perhaps Shue didn't deliberately kill himself? However, the Air Force says, 'We think his choice of the grove of trees reflects his ambivalence about dying that is often present in suicidal persons.' Do they mean he was ambivalent about dying or apathetic about how to do it?

'One could speculate that they (the threatening notes) were motives for telling the insurance company to get the ex-wife's policies cancelled.' Do they mean that the Colonel could have invented these notes as a ploy, especially given that he never went to police about them! Could this mean he had not intended to kill himself; but rather, that he had staged the event as a means by which he might finally get the insurance policy on his life cancelled, by pretending he had been kidnapped and mutilated by the letter writers, who he believed to be his ex-wife and new husband? Was he trying to frame them, to get the policy cancelled? It would seem a bit extreme to go to the extent of cutting off his nipples though, surely?

"There are too many unanswered questions," said Lieutenant Anderson, years after. "They didn't preserve the scene. It wasn't handled as if it had been a crime scene or that a crime took place someplace else. To this day I believe that a crime had been committed to this man prior to that traffic accident. I think he was intercepted on his way to work. I think somebody was laying for him, to take him to some location unknown. I think they intended to terrorize the man. It would appear the Colonel was able to tear away the bonds and get to his vehicle and attempt to escape."

Yet the Colonel had no defensive wounds and his bindings were not at all strained. Oddly, Life magazine reported that in 1978, 'He had told family and friends that a lone gun man in a car shot at him while he was driving home.' Who was this lone gunman? Did the Colonel mean people had been after him for over twenty years? Or did the Colonel spiral into an ever – increasing cycle of paranoia and fantasy?

Did the Colonel fake his own abduction and it went horribly wrong? But if so, what would make him come up with idea of cutting off his nipples and little finger? How could he tie up his hands and feet and yet leave no fingerprints? Where did the lidocaine come from? Why were his contact lenses found on his cheeks? And, did he pull his own ears so hard that they were both torn and hanging down when he was found? Why was one part of his chest shaved? Where were his missing body parts?

Who cut the L-shaped hole in the back pocket of his trousers?

What did happen to Colonel Shue?

Chapter Eight:

The Mystery on Ilkley Moor

On December the 1st 1987, retired Policeman Phillip Spencer set out across the Ilkley Moors in the early hours of the morning. He was walking in a part called Rombalds Moor, just a few miles from where Heathcliff in Emily Brontë's Wuthering Heights wandered tormented in the howling wind. It's a mystical and ancient landscape. These moors have the second highest concentration of ancient stones in Europe, dating back to the Neolithic Age and including a stone circle called The Twelve Apostles, and an ancient pre-Christian Swastika Stone, similar in style to The Camunian Rose, which is located at Woodhouse Crag on the northern edge of Ilkley Moor.

As Mr Spencer set out in the early hours of that morning, he took with him a camera, in the hope of photographing the strange lights that had recently been reported in the area. It was dark and the moors were shrouded in swirling mist and Mr Spencer wondered if he would be able to get any pictures at all, although he had loaded his camera with ultra-light-sensitive film. He walked for a while in silence and as dawn approached fast, the mist began to clear a little. Suddenly, to his immense surprise, he spotted a strange figure up ahead of him in the gloom. Instinct made him reach for his camera and he snapped some shots, one of which would later go down in the annals of the unexplained as one of the most mysterious photos ever taken. Although the photos are slightly blurry, perhaps due to Mr Spencer's understandable shock at what he was seeing, one photo appears to show an upright lumbering figure, later estimated to be approximately one meter tall. Former policeman Spencer would later say that he ran after the creature, until it entered a "dome-shaped craft" which rose rapidly into the sky before Spencer could take a photo of it.

After the strange creature and craft vanished, Mr Spencer walked quickly to his father-in-law's house in the nearby village of East Morton, where he had been heading before the encounter. As he reached the row of houses, he glanced at the village clock. It was an hour fast! Upon entering his father-in-law's house, he saw that the clocks in the house were also an hour fast. As he looked at his wrist-watch, it was also showing the wrong time. Then he stopped to think. He believed that his encounter with the strange fellow on the moors had lasted mere seconds. Now, it appeared he was quite wrong. It appeared that he had lost over an hour of time that he could not account for. Rather unnerved by this, he felt the creeping sensation of fear set in. Had something happened to him on the moor, that had led him to spend an hour longer there than he realized? But if so, what could that be? He got his compass out of his pocket. The compass was now pointing South; yet he knew, that according to where he was, it should be facing North.

Spencer did not delay in taking his roll of film to the nearest photo shop to have it developed, and when it was ready to collect, he looked through the photos. He knew then that his eyes had not deceived him. In one of the photos there was this strange-looking creature, who appeared to be coming down a slight hill about 30 feet away from where Mr Spencer had been standing. The creature was mottled brown and green and grey and it had a huge head. It had a thin body and long spindly legs. Its arms hung almost down to its feet, and its hands were enormous. It looked like it had giant sausages for fingers, thought Mr. Spencer. It almost looked like a giant frog, with some kind of hat on, walking upright! Mr Spencer would later say that it had not walked so much as shuffled along, but that it was moving fast, faster than a human could walk.

A wildlife expert was consulted. Could Mr Spencer have been experiencing Pareidolia? Was it really just a tree stump, a rock, or a bush, and Spencer had been tricked into thinking it looked like a horrifying creature from a scary sci-fi movie? Yet there it was in the photo, and the wildlife expert concluded that whatever was in the photograph was not a bush, a tree, or a stump, and it was not any known animal either.

Mr Spencer contacted 'UFO' researchers Peter Hough and Jenny Randles, who sent the photo off to the Kodak Laboratory in Hemel Hempstead for analysis. The Labs conclusion was that nothing in the photo was superimposed nor was it double exposure, and that the photo had not been tampered with in any way. Bearing in mind of course too that 'photoshopping' was not possible back in the 1970's like it is today, so faking a photograph would have been a lot harder to do too, and the Lab said it was not fake. Investigator Randles said, "I fought against this case in our minds for many years, owing to its intrinsic 'impossibility,' but the bottom line is that you can only present the facts. And in this case, the photo was studied by several photography labs, the physical evidence by two university labs, and the witness by clinical psychologists. Not one of these sources found evidence to challenge the case." In 1989, The Daily Star Newspaper proclaimed that they had "debunked" the photo. They stated that the photo of the strange creature on the moors, was actually an insurance salesman riding his bike across the moors, en-route to a customer's house. Quite why an insurance salesman would be riding a bike across the bleak landscape of the moors in the pre-dawn hours, was not explained! However, it turned out that the newspaper staff were playing a practical joke on each other!

Not long after Mr Spencer's strange encounter, he began to experience strange dreams at night, disturbing dreams. Rather perturbed by this, Mr Spencer decided he should perhaps seek out a regression therapist, to try to get to the bottom of what had happened to him on the moor. A Dr Jim Singleton, clinical psychologist and expert in hypnotherapy and regression, agreed to help.

The session was arranged, and in time, Mr. Spencer began to describe his memories. He said that his encounter with the strange creature happened after he had been 'returned'. He said he had been abducted out on the moor and that when he had snapped the photo, the creature was actually waving "Goodbye" to him! Spencer began to describe how he had been taken aboard a flying object that had taken him up into orbit and then shown him "videos," one of which depicted a coming apocalypse, and the other video, Spencer would not talk about. He said he was "not allowed to disclose the content." What could he have seen? Peter Hough, Jenny Randles' investigative partner, asked the psychologist Dr Singleton to assess Mr. Spencer mentally. Could Spencer be suffering from delusions? Had he gone completely mad? The psychologist stated that in his professional opinion, Mr Spencer was not suffering from any kind of madness and that he appeared to be telling the truth.

Spencer described in vivid detail what he believed happened to him. "I'm walking along the moor. It's windy and there are a lot of clouds. Walking up toward some trees I see this little something; can't tell... He's green and moving toward me... Oh! I'm stuck. I can't move, and the creature is still coming toward me. I'm stuck and everything has gone fuzzy. I'm floating in the air. I want to get down. I can't get down. I don't like it. This green thing is in front of me." Spencer would later say that the creature was in front of him but below him, and that the scene reminded him of when a child is pulling along balloon in the air from a length of string on the ground. "Oh God! I want to get down. There's a big silver saucer thing, there's a door in it. I don't want to go in there. Everything has gone black. I'm in a funny room. A voice is saying, "Don't be afraid." I don't feel afraid. There's a beam above me, fluorescent tube. I don't want to look at it. My nose feels funny. I can see a door and there is one of these green creatures motioning for me to go with him. I don't want to go with him. Oh God! Don't want to be up here!"

"I'm in a big round room. I'm on a raised platform. He says I've got nothing to fear but I'd still like to go home. It's got such big hands. It's so bright. Two of those creatures have come with me. I'm looking at pictures on the wall. Scenes of destruction like on the news. People starving. It's not very nice. Pictures changing, another film. He's asking if I understand. I'm not supposed to tell anyone about the other film. It's time to go. Everything is black. I'm walking up the moor again, near some trees. I see something. A creature. I've shouted to it. I don't know what it is. It's moving quick. I'll photograph it. I'm running after it. It's got big eyes, pointed ears. Hasn't got a nose. His hands are enormous. Three big fingers. Its arms are long. Looks odd. Funny feet – V-shape, two toes. Must be difficult to walk – he shuffles along. It's gone round a corner....' And then it is gone.

One crucial fact came out of this session. The only problem that had existed with the photo, when it had been analysed, other than of course the inability to identify what the creature was, was that the light conditions seemed to imply that the photograph had not been taken in the early morning as Mr Spencer had said. There was more daylight in the photo than would have been expected. However, the sessions confirmed that the photo had been taken one hour later than Spencer had thought, and it would have been lighter then.

The former policeman's account never wavered, never changed. He sought out no publicity, though his story would inevitably come out, nor did he make any financial gain from his exposure. In fact, he tried to stay as anonymous as possible; and why would a sensible former officer of the law, presumably a rational and logical and sensible man, wish to jeopardise his sterling reputation to become a laughing stock for inevitable sceptics?

Spencer's story doesn't end there. A few weeks after his experience, he was at home when he heard a knock at the door. Upon opening the door, he found two men standing on his doorstep. They were both dressed in black and looked surprisingly alike. They said they were from the Ministry of Defence and flashed some i.d. cards at him. They said their names were Jefferson and Davis, and they asked to come in. Mr Spencer was a little surprised at this, as he certainly had not told the Ministry of Defence about his encounter. On entering his living room, one of the men looked at his electric fire and asked him, "How does this work?" Then, the men announced that they had come to talk to him about the incident on the Moor. Again, this surprised Mr Spencer as he had only told three people about what he'd experienced that early morning in the mist, and the three people he had told had no connection whatsoever to any Government departments. However, these two men appeared to know all the details about it. Mr Spencer wasn't sure what to say to them, but given that they were saying they were from the Government, he thought he ought to just to be honest, and so he gave a short account of his experience and said that he had taken a photograph.

At this, the two men themselves appeared to be very surprised. When they discovered that a photograph existed, they were quick to ask for it, but Spencer explained to them that it was not in his possession, but rather, that it was with a friend. Actually, it wasn't, but Mr Spencer had come to the conclusion that there was something about these men, and he did not want to hand his photo over to them. After he told them he did not have it, they seemed to lose interest very fast, and they got up to leave.

After they had gone, Mr Spencer telephoned the Ministry of Defence, as well as the Air Force to enquire about who these two men were. He gave their names and described them; but Mr Spencer was told that no such men existed.

Of his strange adventure, Spencer said, "I feel I have been dropped into a sea of uncertainty. What happened to me on the moor was too impossible. It throws everything which you think is normal, certain and secure into question. I now exist in a vacuum of disbelief, occasionally reaching out to hold onto something solid, only to discover it is a hologram."

Who was the strange creature? And where did he come from? What makes Spencer's story all the more interesting, is that seven years earlier on 16th of June 1980, a short way away on Ilkley Moor near Todmorden, 56-year old coal miner Zigmund Adamski was found dead lying on top of a coal pile over twenty miles from his home in Tingley, with an ointment covering a wound which no lab could identify. The coroner ruled he had "died of fright."

Chapter Nine:

The Missing Body Parts

'A potential and unusual murder mystery 2,000 miles away has left a family with many heart-breaking questions,' wrote the Mableton News in 2013. 'A mother is looking for answers about her son's death.' In July 2013 Ryan Singleton was found dead in the desert of Death Valley, his organs missing. Ryan Singleton, 24, was a handsome young man, and he had left his home in Atlanta, Georgia to pursue his dreams of making it big as a model and actor. He had gained some success, once landing a spot on the New York Fashion Week runway. He'd settled in New York City and married a celebrity fashion stylist, Kyhte Brewster, a man more than twice his age who styled stars like Beyoncé. Their marriage lasted only four months however. It seems that at the time of Ryan's death, he had moved back home to his mother's in Atlanta. EXIA reporter Phillip Kosh spoke to his mother. 'Ryan Singleton wanted to be a Star, his mother remembers. "I saw on Facebook where he was walking down the runway Fashion Week with a pair of gold shorts on. I'm like, alright, he is doing what he wants to do," then Ryan set his sights on Hollywood. He and some friends packed their stuff into a U-Haul truck and drove west to Los Angeles. They documented their journey along the way for a docu-series.' After some time, Ryan left L.A. and moved back to New York. "I find out on social media Ryan has gotten married to a man twice his age," said his mother. "I don't have a clue what's going on." Then the couple split. As for Ryan's documentary, PRS Newswire described it as, 'Documentary turns into horror movie when Star is murdered.' T.D. Faison, one of Ryan's partners on the documentary said, "We were going to become the next biggest film producers out there just like HBO's Entourage.... it just didn't play out like that!" Their dream was ended by the mysterious disappearance of Ryan.

Ryan's mother Iris Flowers told reporter Kosch of an 'ominous conversation she had with her son after he moved back. "Something bad is going to happen to me isn't it?" Ryan asked her. "Ryan, what are you talking about?" Iris asked her son if he owed someone money and he said no. "I've done a lot of things to hurt a lot of people," Ryan replied. Iris said she never found out exactly what Ryan was talking about. "I don't know if he felt some kind of way because he left the (production) team, married Kythe and it didn't work out with Kythe and now he's home. He knew he hurt me by disappearing and not communicating with me. Anybody outside of that, I couldn't figure out who it could be." Two days later, Ryan abruptly left for Los Angeles again. This was the last time Iris saw her son alive. After Ryan disappeared, his mother said she got a call from his husband, who she said told her that Ryan had called him and it seemed like he had been drinking. She said Kythe told her that Ryan's life could be in danger.' 74 days later, his body was found in the desert of Death Valley.

According to Ryan's autopsy report from the San Bernardino's County Sheriff's Department Coroner Division, on July the 6th 2013 Ryan flew to Los Angeles to stay with a friend. The following day, July the 7th, he left for Las Vegas. On July the 8th he called his friend in LA to say he was on his way back from Las Vegas. At 22 hours that night, he called the same friend and said he was going to pull over and get some sleep. The following day, on July the 9th, he called his friend to say he was running low on gas and food. His friend transferred $60 into Ryan's bank account. His mother said he called her and asked her to send him $100 via Western Union to Nevada. Around 3 pm that day, Ryan called his friend again to ask him if he could come and pick him up near Baker. His friend agreed and set off for the 3-hour drive to reach Ryan. Earlier that day, a highway patrol officer reported that he'd spotted Ryan walking along the highway, Interstate 15. The patrolman said Ryan told him he was looking for his car and that he'd been attacked by small animals. The patrol officer said he did not believe Mr. Ryan was under the influence of drink or drugs. The patrolman told Ryan to get into his patrol car and they drove along the highway looking for Ryan's rental car, but could not find it. Presumably it had run out of petrol? In the end, the patrol officer dropped Ryan at the rest stop and gas station in Baker and it was from here that Ryan had phoned his friend. Somehow, between that phone call and his friend arriving to pick him up, Ryan vanished. Almost three months later, what was left of Ryan's body was found by two men who had gone out into the desert surrounding the rest stop to hike.

It took a while for Ryan's autopsy results to be released, and his case was sent to "The Special Case Division." The San Bernardino County Coroner's Office said, "There is no cause of death. The body was severely decomposed, animals might have been involved. The case has been sent to the special case division because it deserves more attention than we can give it." This only fuelled suspicion that this was not a natural death. His body was found approximately 2 miles from the rest stop where the patrolman had dropped him off. Temperatures in Death Valley reach 120 degrees. There is very little shelter in this barren, scorching landscape that is one of the most hostile places on earth. Why would Ryan leave the only shelter there was inside the rest stop, to walk almost two miles to where his body was later found? Who in their right mind would even consider doing such a thing? And yet, the patrolman certainly believed Ryan was in his right mind. When the patrolman met up with Ryan, he had by this time, according to where his abandoned rental car was later found, already walked over two miles in the overwhelming heat. The patrolman found Ryan to be in a normal mental condition, but could he have been suffering from dehydration having walked so far already? Had his mind become cloudy and confused as a result, and after calling his friend at the rest stop, had he wandered off into the desert in a state of delirium? Yet, the patrolman for one didn't see anything wrong with him. On the other hand, isn't it a bit odd to say that small animals are attacking you? What kind of little animals could Ryan have meant? Are there any little animals in the desert? There are snakes, coyotes, but what else is there? Was he really in his right mind? Or did he simply mean insects, rather than animals?

What could make Ryan leave the only shelter there was, when he knew his friend was on his way to pick him up? Even stranger was that at this popular stopping point of a heavily trafficked route between Las Vegas and Los Angeles, a place at which many travellers stop to fill up on gas and to purchase refreshments; nobody recalled seeing him there, nor seeing him wandering off into the desert. Professor Joseph Scott Morgan of Jackson State University, a professor of forensics who reviewed the case for 11 Five News, asks, "How does someone just disappear in an area where you have so few places to go? The curious thing about this is you have no-where to hide, no-where to seek shelter other than a man-made structure," and the only man-made structure around for miles was the rest stop and buildings there. "It's like a moon -scape. Someone in their right mind would say, this is not healthy for me. I don't need to be out in this. Why would they wander off to succumb to this environment?" Over a mile and a half is a considerable distance to walk in such terrific heat, and where was he heading when it was a path to only the desert? Had someone led him away? Or, had he been taken away and his body returned at a later time? His ex-husband said, "I believe that he was taken from there, and later put back there. I just don't think he passed out there and was there for two and a half months." Perhaps it was a twisted serial killer, and Ryan just happened to be in the wrong place at the right time? Or had there been some kind of targeting involved? Had Ryan become a victim not randomly but because of who he was? His ex-husband wondered if Ryan had been targeted for his openly gay lifestyle. Why Ryan believed he was in danger, and from whom, has never been revealed. His death was classified as "undetermined," with no mention of any foul play involved. But if there was foul play, as his mother and ex-husband believe, why did no-one notice anything suspicious at the rest stop, like a man who looked like he was under duress? Or being coerced? Then again, a serial killer can look very innocent and harmless. Think of Ted Bundy, who easily managed to lure female victims unwittingly to help him put his groceries in his car. He pretended to have a broken arm. Perhaps Ryan was asked to help a driver or trucker, who played a fake victim too, to suck Ryan in and then drive off with him. Certainly though, it doesn't make sense that Ryan would have willingly got into a vehicle when he knew his friend was on his way to collect him. He didn't need to accept a ride from a stranger.

His mother said police told her there was video surveillance of her son being in the store at the gas station. His mother has said in TV interviews, "My son was six-foot-five and he was chocolate and he was a lifeguard before he left Georgia to go to California for the weekend so I don't understand why you're telling me that no-one saw my child? Nothing?"

But it gets stranger. When Ryan's body was found 74 days later, his mother was horrified. She could not understand what she was being told. She said, "There were no eyes, no heart, no lungs and no kidney." These details led to a frenzy online, not only from mainstream media news channels. There were many who speculated that Ryan had fallen victim to illegal organ trafficking.

One YouTube channel, 'AfriSynergy,' said that Ryan was an African-American, "and a kidney on the black market sells for over $60,000. Lungs even more. These are a group of people who are feasting on young black people. This is what is going on. A vampire-type behaviour. These were people who believe that they deserve your organs more than you deserve your organs. When they look at you, they are looking at an extended life; what they would like to have for themselves: eternity. Especially with these melanated organs." Melanin is a distinct chemical in the body that gives darker skin its pigmentation. "Melanated" is an adjective form of melanin that has been coined in more recent years by some in the African American community. There is an esoteric meaning behind this. A Dr. Jewel Pookrum says, "Melanin is the face of the Universe/ God." It's produced in the pineal gland, where the 3rd eye is said to exist. The third eye is said to be the doorway to clairvoyance and psychic abilities, miracles and the divine realm of the God spirit, and supernatural powers. People with darker skin tone produce higher quantities of Melanin in the 3rd eye, some believe. Melanin secretes into the blood stream. This has led to the controversial conspiracy theory that certain elite wealthy people seek the organs and pineal glands of darker skinned people to feast upon; including "melanin harvesting" so it can be injected, in order to gain these third eye powers and to extend their years in the pursuit of eternal life. Secret Societies like The Skull and Bones, of which many US politicians have belonged, these conspiracy theorists believe, eat "live" pineal glands during ceremonies, to gain greater occult power. Some say the pineal glands of the ancient Egyptians would be eaten in the years before Christ.

Ryan's autopsy report, which was released in September 2013, states that his body was badly decomposed and mostly skeletal when it was discovered. Several bones appear to have been 'disarticulated from the body by animal activity. No internal organs of the chest, abdomen, or pelvis, secondary to animal activity,' and 'most of the ribs of the left chest have been removed by animal activity. No onsite trauma was discovered at the scene. His organs are missing because animals took them, the autopsy report says. His mother disagrees. "I just cannot believe some animal came to my son's body and opened it up very precisely and removed just the eyes, heart, lungs, liver and kidneys and his whole body was remarkably intact when he was found. For my son to be found with his shoes, his socks, shorts, fully dressed and remarkably intact and you want me to believe animals?"

Ryan still had his shoes, socks, shorts; they were not ripped apart by animals scavenging, although the autopsy says his shorts were 'deteriorated. "Either his clothes were ripped or they weren't," said Sheryl McCollum, founder and director of the Cold Case Investigative Research Institute in Atlanta. "We have a lot of questions. I think that it may have been some kind of illicit team or organization in that city and to me it felt completely like Ryan walked out of that store, somebody took him and hit him in the head and put him in the back of a truck against his will and he was still in that city. That was the first thing I felt when the detective called me and said Ryan was a missing person. Singleton's autopsy report lists 'possible' trauma to side of head. Mrs. Flowers says that when his rental car was searched, any fingerprints had been wiped clean. If his organs were removed by animals, explain it to her. Either those bones have got gnaw marks from an animal or they don't." His mother said she phoned to ask, "Was his body dismembered? Were parts of his body strewn all over…near where he was found?" "No," the voice on the other end of the phone said. Not a single limb had been severed, like one would expect from a wild animal attack. Not a leg, not an arm or hand… nothing was ripped from his body," said his mother. "This explanation of coyotes apparently being discriminate on what they took and did not take – was too far-fetched to accept," she said to NDTV news.

No matter how horrifying to consider, his mother cannot help but wonder if his organs were taken from his body to be sold. He was a healthy, fit, young man; the perfect specimen. "How long was he out in the desert? He was missing for 74 days before I go that phone call. For me it feels like murder. It feels like someone took my son and killed him and took his organs. For his body not to be strewn about if animals did this, just does not add up." His eyes, kidney, heart, liver, lungs; all were gone. But these are all soft organs. Couldn't the coyotes and vultures have, no matter how dreadful to think about it, have eaten them? Or was it something far more sinister?

When Ryan's tragic story first came out, Fox News spoke with Professor Nancy Scheper – Hughes, the founder of 'Organs Watch.' It's an organisation that investigates illegal organ trafficking and tracks suspected activities. In the past they have uncovered operations including one such case in 2009, which led to a number of arrests in New York, New Jersey and Israel. Professor in the department of Anthropology at the University of California, Berkeley, Nancy Scheper-Hughes writes in an essay published in The Lancet in 2003, 'In general, the circulation of kidneys follows established routes from South to North, from East to West, from poorer to more affluent bodies, from black and brown bodies to white ones, and from poor low status men to more affluent men. We have observed and interviewed hundreds of transplant surgeons who practise or facilitate illicit surgeries with purchased organs, we have met with organ brokers and their criminal links. In one well-travelled route, small groups of transplant patients go by charter plane to Turkey where they are matched with kidney sellers from rural Moldova and Romania and are transplanted by a team of surgeons. One network unites European and North American patients with Philippine kidney sellers in a private episcopal hospital in Manila, arranged through an independent internet broker who advertises via websites.'

Pacific Standard Magazine calls Scheper – Hughes 'The Organ Detective.' 'In the U.S., the waiting list for a kidney now stretches past 100,000 people, while the rate of donations has remained relatively flat for the past decade or so. The WHO estimates that one in 10 of all those transplanted organs was procured on the black market. In today's global market an Indian kidney fetches as little as $1000, a Filipino kidney can get $1300, a Moldovan or Romanian kidney yields $2700. Sellers in the USA can receive up to $30,000.' The thing is, Ryan Singleton, though poor at the time of his disappearance, was not from a poverty-stricken country where it would seem that most donors are found. It seems that the most prevalent countries the black-market organs are obtained from are where people live in far greater poverty than the United Sates; although, from the statistics above, it also appears that an American organ is worth far more money than a third world one. It would seem wholly outlandish to suggest that Ryan was abducted and operated on for his kidneys; and yet, apparently, they would fetch an awful lot of money if he had been.

But how would a member or members of an established trafficking network just happen to be passing and seize on the chance of taking someone like Ryan at a rest stop? Organ extraction requires highly sterile and surgical conditions which were certainly not available at the rest stop and yet, could they have driven him to such a place?

Perhaps a very wealthy client nearby had an urgent need for a kidney or a different organ, and was prepared to pay a lot of money for an urgent delivery? And Ryan served that very pressing need? Yet surely, there are more populated places to look than in Death Valley? Like in the heart of Vegas, rather than along the Highway at a rest stop, although it is the main thoroughfare from Las Vegas to LA so the rest stop is not a quiet spot. Yet if this had been the case, why bring his body back to the spot at which he disappeared? Unless their intention was to make it look just as it did to the authorities: That he had somehow died 'naturally' in the desert after succumbing to the heat and his body had lain there all that time. His body had become almost mummified, so certainly he had been lying in the desert for a long time; but had he been returned there after being taken somewhere first?

If an organ is harvested for transplant however, it has to be an HLA match to the recipient. In other words, not just anyone's organs will be compatible, and compatibility testing needs to take place before the organs are extracted. How would an organ trafficker know in advance if Ryan's organs would be compatible? It seems implausible that a black-market organ harvesting ring would snatch a random person at a gas station, kill him, harvest his organs, and just hope to find a rich person with failing organs who matched Ryan's organs, within a few hours before the organs deteriorated? Nancy Scheper-Hughes said, "There are a lot easier ways to get tissue."

Ryan's autopsy listed his cause of death as 'Undetermined due to advanced decomposition.' Professor of Forensics Joseph Scott Morgan of Jacksonville State University appraised Ryan's autopsy report and compared it with that of another very controversial case, 17-year-old Kendrick Johnson, who died at his school in Georgia in January 2013. When Kendrick did not return home from school one day, his body was eventually found in a wrapped-up gym mat. It was determined that Kendrick had climbed inside the rolled-up mat to retrieve his sports shoe and become stuck and died of suffocation. When his parents hired a private pathologist to review their son's case, the pathologist discovered that all of Kendrick's internal organs had been removed and replaced with stuffed newspaper. Kendrick's family also believed it was possible that their son's organs had been sold. In Ryan's case Professor Morgan said, "That means you would have to have smooth margins that indicates a scalpel has opened the body. There's no indication of that. As a matter of fact, there's little or no tissue that's left on the outside of the body." On the other hand, because there is very little tissue left on Ryan's skeletal remains, perhaps one could offer the suggestion that this was the plan all along – to extract Ryan's organs and dump his body back in the desert where the animals would come and pick at it, removing the evidence of a scalpel in his tissue by removing the tissue! However, I am not a forensic expert and perhaps this is just a silly suggestion. But if the tissue was gone, so too would be the scalpel marks used to open the body up to take the internal organs out, wouldn't they? A counter argument to this would be that if his organs had been stolen, why would he still be wearing his clothes?

On another point, strangely, Snopes journalists said they found no record of any patrol officer escorting Ryan Singleton to the rest-stop. 'Singleton was allegedly dropped off by a CHP (California Highway Patrol officer,) following an unsuccessful search for his rental car. However, officials with both the CHP and NHP (Nevada Highway Patrol) told us that they have no record of

Singleton's interacting with members of their department.' An NHP spokesperson said that their officers would not drive anyone across state lines in the manner described by reports.' Well, that's strange.

Could there be a more rational cause for Ryan's death other than organ trafficking? Did the answer lie closer to home? Could someone Ryan knew personally or professionally have had some kind of beef with him, to the point that they would come to where he was and do something to him? Or had they sent someone to do something to him? Had Ryan got into money trouble? He'd borrowed from his mother and friend on the day he vanished. Had he blown his last dollars in Vegas and now he owed money to the wrong kind of people? – Yet Ryan didn't even have enough money to gamble, did he? Had he borrowed more money from the wrong kind of people? Or, had his money problems driven him to do something he wouldn't normally consider, something dangerous? Like drug smuggling? Had he got into something he couldn't get out of, and now bad people were after him? Why did Ryan tell his mother he had hurt people and he was in trouble? Yet there were no signs of foul play and no clues at the scene. And, how did they kill him, if he was murdered?

Did Ryan, broke and jobless, feel like his life was a failure? He hadn't made it big. Did frustration lead to mounting depression and desperation, which led to suicidal thoughts? Was he overcome with shame or guilt? He told his mother he had hurt people. Did he walk into the desert to die? Or did he simply get bored and restless waiting three hours for his friend to arrive and he wandered off and became overcome by the heat? Was it just a tragic accident? Yet he had already walked two miles from his rental car and survived that before the cop stopped to pick him up, or didn't, according to which version we are to believe.

Could Ryan have been under the influence of drugs, willingly or unwittingly, and the patrol officer, if he did exist, had simply not realized? Ryan had left his cell phone in his rental car. Did he ask someone at the rest stop to help him find his rental car because he wanted to go and get it? Police did later find his cell phone in the car. His fingerprints were wiped; which is odd. Did a hypothetical person he asked for a ride, turn out to be a bad person? Had Ryan been attacked, perhaps from behind? His autopsy did mention 'possible' trauma to the head; 'indications of haemorrhaging of the brain.' Ryan's autopsy says 'The outer layer of the brain is stained dark red, suggesting some superficial haemorrhage,' and 'the skull underneath the dura on the left side is pale, suggesting a possible haemorrhage on the left side.' Also, 'A fracture line is noted on the lateral wall of the left temporal fossa.' However, the pathologist also notes, 'the fractural line begins or ends at one of the saw cuts, so it may be an autopsy artefact.' And, 'The inner aspect of the fractured bone was examined by the undersigned forensic anthropologist. There was no evidence of decompositional material within the left temporal bone fracture line, suggesting it did not occur prior to the body decomposing.' In other words, this fracture to the head happened after death, not before. Could he have been killed in a different manner, such as strangulation perhaps? Ryan have been killed by a roaming serial killer? It's not unknown for a serial killer to mutilate or even take body parts, as a sick trophy or as keepsakes.

Could someone else have been in the rental car when it ran out of gas? But if so, where was this person when the cop pulled over to give Ryan a ride to the gas station? Although the autopsy report says animals attacked Ryan's body, strangely, no gnawing marks or clawing or bite marks from animals were noted, however it did say 'due to animals.' For example, 'All soft tissue of the upper forearm on the right-hand side is missing by animal activity,' and, 'The left upper extremity is nearly completely disarticulated from the body.' Does this mean animals pulled his body around? 'There are possibly what might have been athletic shorts.' So, had they degraded or been torn off or pulled by animals?

Perhaps the Medical Examiner did not feel the need to expand upon this in further detail? Although of course, if so, this doesn't mean something wasn't done to Ryan's body before the animals got there.

There is something else however, beyond all of this, which is even stranger. Ryan's mother said, "The coroner's report stated no tattoos were found on Ryan: but he had tattoos." She said on TV, "When I read the report it said tattoos - none were found, and I'm like "Wait a minute. My son had tattoos, so now you're telling me that animals came and removed his organs. Were these animals smart enough to go and remove the tattoos as well?" How do you explain that? Because to me it's like somebody removed his tattoos so he couldn't be identified. Those are identifiable marks. I have a lot of questions. For my son to be found with his shoes, his socks, shorts, fully dressed and remarkably intact and you want me to believe, animals…. ?"

Her son was found with his shoes still on, his socks still on, but he no longer had any tattoos…. What did happen to Ryan Singleton?

Chapter Ten:

The mystery of the Silver Elves & the missing Man

In December 1998, 23-year-old Matthew David Pendergrast was in his last semester at Rhodes College, Tennessee. On the morning he disappeared, he'd been due at class, a distance of four blocks away from his apartment. That morning, he left his apartment in Memphis, but he never arrived at class. That same day, his Toyota vehicle was found abandoned on a private levee near Bayou Meta swamp, off Kerr Road in Lonoke County, Arkansas, off Interstate 40. This is a distance of approximately 125 kilometres from his apartment.

His vehicle was found on private land that is reserved for duck hunters. One of the hunters who found his vehicle, Joe Murdall, told Matthew's mother Mary Ellen that he and a friend had seen her son's SUV parked there at around 2 pm. He said it had not been there when they passed the area at 10 a.m. that morning.

The hunters said they'd left a note on the windshield of the vehicle, asking for the owner to move it. The next day, the two hunters saw the vehicle was still there, and it was then that they looked inside the vehicle for some i.d. The vehicle was unlocked and they noticed that the keys were still in the ignition. In the glove compartment, they found an old oil change receipt and it had Matthew's parent's phone number on it. A backpack was sitting inside the vehicle. It was later identified as the backpack Matthew used for college.

When the police arrived, they searched the area. The following day they found Matthew's blue jeans, and in the back pocket was his wallet containing his driver's license, credit card and $46 in cash. His jeans were approximately 100 yards from his abandoned vehicle, inside a wooded thicket. Along with his jeans, placed in a neat pile were his T-shirt, shoes and socks. There was no sign of Matthew however. When the police looked more closely at Matthew's clothes, they discovered that his trousers were wet from the knees down, and the way they were left, it looked like Matthew had stepped out of them and dropped them to the floor where he stood. Although his trousers were soaking wet, one of the investigators on the scene remarked that his T-shirt was as dry "as if it had just come out of the dryer." Although it was winter, no jacket was found.

Matthew had driven way-off course on the morning of his disappearance, driving 125 miles for some reason, and then turning off the main highway and driving down a private dirt road that led only to a swamp and a levee. It would seem that he had then taken off all his clothes and shoes and vanished, or so it would appear.

As for the rest of the story, or at least those parts that are known, it will involve the curious and often inexplicable actions of a cast of characters including silver Elves, a Hitman in a Cadillac, an Elvis impersonator, and a somewhat strange home invasion.

Matthew was last seen leaving his residence in Memphis between 7:30 a.m. and 8:00 a.m., on December the 1st 2000 in his SUV which had Georgia license plates. His landlady later said that she heard him moving around just before this time. The previous evening, Matthew had appeared in a play on campus. After that, back at his apartment, he had called a friend in Atlanta to discuss what he would write in an upcoming college paper. His friend, Geo Presley-Brookes said he was upbeat when they talked. Early the following morning, Matthew had sent a text to the same friend saying; "Everything's all right. No problem. I'll talk to you later." Some wondered, what did this message mean? Was it some kind of clue about what had happened to Matthew, or what he was planning to do? And yet, is perhaps the most obvious answer that after speaking to his friend he had continued working on his college paper or run it through in his mind, and was now sure how he would write his college paper, and Matthew was letting his friend know? Or, maybe there was something else going on?

Matthew was Caucasian, five feet six inches and slim, with Brown hair and blue eyes. He had dimples in his cheeks. He was sociable and well-liked. He played in the college soccer team and he'd wrestled at the private school he attended in Atlanta before coming to college in Memphis. He liked to play tennis. He ran track and cross-country. At college he joined the Kappa Sigma fraternity. He enjoyed playing a Multi-User Dungeons and Dragons game online called Threshold-RPG.

When his parents received the call from the two hunters about their son's abandoned vehicle, they immediately began to co-ordinate a search from their home in Georgia. First, they phoned the campus security. Security guards checked Matthew's apartment and then issued an email to all students asking for anyone who knew his whereabouts to contact them. Meanwhile, over the next few days, searches were carried out at the bayou. Helicopters flew over the swamp and woods with night vision equipment, and divers with sonar equipment entered the water. Bloodhounds, then cadaver dogs were brought in. The K-9 team picked up Matthew's scent from his pile of clothes in the woods and it lead them to the edge of Bayou Meto, then away again. Bayou Meto is a huge state-owned wildlife management area, comprising 30,000 acres and much of it is flooded. The river is a complex waterway that winds through five Arkansas counties. Next to the bayou is thick woodland.

What perplexed his parents was that Matthew was never known as a camper or hiker. His parents and the investigators too, could see no obvious attraction for Matt to be here. Strangely, although the dogs picked up the young man's scent from the pile of clothes to the edge of Bayou Meto, they found no scent to follow from his vehicle to his clothes. There were also no footprints. How did he get from his vehicle to where his clothes were found, without leaving any footprints or a scent? Investigators also found no signs of anyone being with him; no signs of a struggle, no weapons, nor any DNA evidence. When Matthew's clothing was found, his mother expressed the opinion that it appeared to be possible this scene was staged. Her son, she said, was not a particularly tidy young man, so she couldn't imagine him placing his clothes down in such a neat pile. His bedroom at home was notoriously untidy, she explained, so she did not feel this was the work of her son. His mother felt there was something sinister about all this. Matthew's friend Jason Woods stayed in the search area for nearly two weeks, and he claimed that the searchers, "Walked all round the scene with disregard and flew around on ATV's, mucking up the scents, footprints, all manner of potential evidence around the car, the levee, the woods. They didn't even search the trailer park beyond the far bank of the stream." What was odd was that to get to the woods where Matthew's clothes were found, he would have had to wade through a drainage ditch where the water was over waist-high, but his scent was not detected there.

The police meanwhile were wondering, had Matthew perhaps committed suicide? It's sadly quite common for those who tragically take their own lives, by walking into rivers or the sea, to take off their clothes and place them in a neat pile before wading into the water. Could Matthew have done this? Yet divers looked for his body and they could not find it. It was not a fast-flowing river either.

Matthew had been described as "upbeat" during his phone call in the early hours before he disappeared. He'd enjoyed performing in the play the night before, and we know he was planning a paper that was soon due. He was actively sociable at university, belonged to several clubs and had many friends. It would seem he had no known problems that could have led him to be suicidally depressed. His mother said, "He was a little worried about papers he had due, to finish up his degree, but other than that he was in good spirits. He was an excited young man who was looking forward to graduating. He had plans of starting his own non-profit organization to help those in need in Third World countries. So, he was looking forward like he had a bright future, with direction and meaning in his life." She also added, "If Matt were interested in some type of respite or retreat, he would have gone to the mountains. We are unaware of any knowledge he might have had of this particular area."

One strange clue was discovered by the police. When Matthew was not studying or playing soccer or tennis, he found great enjoyment playing an interactive online fantasy game of 'Dungeons and Dragons,' and the investigators discovered that this online game had a curious link to something found in his abandoned vehicle. A journal had been found inside Matthew's vehicle and it contained poetry he'd written. The poems were contemplations on life, and nature, and death, with some entries describing 'The Silver Elves.' He wrote about 'Silver Elves' and of seeking 'Immortality,' and of 'walking into water and becoming one with nature again.' What did he mean by this? Did he really mean suicide?

Was he being creative or literal? His parents said there was no way their son would simply walk into the water and drown himself.

It seemed that these journal entries had been inspired from a link on the online game he played to a website called 'The Silver Elves.' On this website was 'The Elven Tree of Life and Death.' It explained that The Silver Elves are a family of Elves who have been living and sharing the Elven Way since 1975, 'and if you choose to, its says, 'you can go on a Journey; The Elven Tree of Life Eternal, known to men as the Tree of Life and Death,' which, 'Reveals the pathways to Faerie and the means to obtaining Immortality, which some seem to think is the doom of the Elves even while they hunger after it.' Did they really mean, a person could become immortal? Or travel to a land where elves and fairies lived? They say, 'The journey begins here. We start here at the bottom of the tree, the ever-present NOW. This is the place of the earth, symbolized by the cross (time/space) in the circle (eternity).' This mysterious group offers you the chance to discover if you are 'An Elf, Faerie, or Otherkin,' and says, 'We will share with you the philosophy, magic and lifestyle of being elven. Elfin is like a secret garden in the midst of the wild and potentially dangerous realm that is Faerie. You are perfectly safe in Elfin but it may take a great deal of courage to pass through Faierie to get there.'

This strongly reminds me of the true tragic tale of Netty Fornario, who also went in search of the Faery realm, only to be found dead on the moors on the barren Island of Iona; her toes bloodied and her face a death-mask of terror.

She'd been trying to make contact with the Faery realm, despite the stern warnings of her wise occultist friends, of the danger it would put her life in. Reporter Marilyn Sadler of Memphis Magazine said one entry in Matthew's journal described, 'The cold mud in the woods, lying down in the icy water, and feeling his blood turning to ice crystals.' Had Matthew tragically believed he could join the Elves and the Fairies by immersing himself in the river? Had he really thought that by drowning himself, this could bring him immortality? Yet drowning deliberately is notoriously difficult to do – the body naturally fights against it in an instinctive need for survival.

Perhaps, rather surprisingly, after Matthew's journal was found, Lonoke County Sheriff's department decided to hire a psychic, Carol Pate, to assist them. 'The psychic claimed that he wanted to be rebirthed as a Silver Elf. The psychic said she "saw" Matt take off his clothes, fold them neatly, and step out into the bayou, where he died of hypothermia.' In other words, he didn't drown himself, but simply passively lay down to die in the cold mud, she determined. But if so, where was his body? The psychic told KATV rather dramatically in a later interview that she believed Matthew "Felt that he was in a battle for his soul, that he was battling demons and he lost."

His mother and his closest friends however, all said that Matthew would never do a thing so crazy as to willingly wade into the muddy water at a random spot off a Highway, and lay down there to die. There was also no evidence that he had ever been a drug taker or was under the influence of some kind of hallucinogenic.

Could his journal writing have simply been role-play for his online character? Was he fleshing-out the character of an elf for his game? Some have suggested that perhaps Matthew could have ingested the drug DMT, an hallucinogenic tryptamine drug that occurs naturally in many plants and animals. It is often referred to as the "spirit molecule" because of the intense psychedelic experience it causes. DMT can be inhaled, ingested, or injected. It causes hallucinations or some say, it opens up the mind's eye to what is really all around us. Ethnobotanist Terrance McKenna, who spent many years studying the effects of DMT, believes that reality is layered with all sorts of dimensions, and DMT simply allows its user to see some of them. When you take it, there is said to be an overwhelming sense that you are entering into an alternate universe that feels 'more real than real.' "At about minute one or two of a DMT trip," according to McKenna, "One may burst through a chrysanthemum-like mandala, and find: There's a whole bunch of entities waiting on the other side, saying "How wonderful that you're here! You come so rarely! We're so delighted to see you!" They come pounding toward you and they will stop in front of you and vibrate, but then they do a very disconcerting thing, which is they jump into your body and then they jump back out again and the whole thing is going on in a high-speed mode where you're being presented with thousands of details per second and you can't get a hold on them, and these things are saying "Don't give in to astonishment", which is exactly what you want to do. You want to go nuts with how crazy this is, and they say, "Pay attention to what we're doing!" It's common for people to see elves, gnomes, and goblins while under the influence of DMT. McKenna says, "You break into this space and are immediately swarmed by squeaking, self-transforming elf-machines, made of light and sound that come chirping and squealing and tumbling toward you. Each "elf creature" elbows others aside, says "Look at this, take this, choose me!" They come toward you, and they offer things to you. You realize what you're being shown — this proliferation of elf gifts, or celestial toys, which seem somehow alive and is "impossible." What they're doing is making objects with their voices, singing structures into existence. It's not simply intricate, beautiful and hard to manufacture, it's impossible to make these things. The toys themselves appear to be somehow alive and can sing other objects into existence, and they're saying, "Do what we are doing!" One user of DMT, a woman called Jodie said, "It was like time travelling, but it wasn't time before or after, it was just adjacent to us. Your bodies were, like, singing – everything you were doing was like a song. You were making a symphony. All these crazy geometric patterns. It seemed like they were laughing at me. Then there were these little elf things. They were letting me know that they were there. I felt very happy, like, "Yeah, this is where I'm supposed to be." Is it possible that Matthew wanted to meet the elves too? But, if he had taken any drugs, why would he have chosen this spot? It was unremarkable and believed to be an unknown area to Matthew. It was also a week day, a day in which he had lectures. Why would he choose to go on an adventure during a college day? His friend Jason Woods told Memphis Magazine, "He wrote creatively about all aspects of life. Focusing on dark poems or fantastical ideas only sensationalizes. Give Matt privacy of thought and a modicum of respect." In other words, his friend's opinion was that it was ludicrous and disrespectful to imply that Matthew's disappearance had anything to do with Elves. His family and friends all believed it was highly unlikely Matthew would have taken any hallucinogenic drugs.

The authorities searched for a week after his neat pile of clothes were found in the thicket. They came up with nothing. No clues at all to explain where Matthew was. All they could do was try to come up with ideas and theories. Lonoke County Sheriff investigator Jim Kulesa believed it was possible the clothes had been staged. But staged by who? And why? And where were their footprints? Matthew had no history of criminal activity or of fraternizing with criminals. His parents wondered had he been kidnapped? Yet no ransom note ever came. In fact, as the weeks turned into years, both the investigators and the family began to believe that the most plausible theory involved a carjacking back in Memphis. The Pendergrasts later described the scenario, as explained to them by police, to have involved a man from Arkansas who was extremely mentally disturbed. The scenario is that this man was on a night of heavy drinking with some friends, getting rowdy, and his friends left him stranded in Memphis "desperate to get back." The theory is that the man then somehow connected with Matthew. Perhaps Matthew offered him a ride or was forced into giving him a ride? Who this man was, and whether he was real or just hypothetical, was never revealed, and eventually the case went cold. That was until 2013, when Matthew Mershon of KATV news announced; 'A possible break in the case.' It came when a mysterious letter was sent to the Jacksonville Police Department. The letter named individuals in a group of people allegedly involved in a missing persons case, and the letter writer believed these people could also be involved in Matthew's disappearance. The original investigator Jim Kulesa and investigators from the Lonoke County Sheriff's department P.D. joined forces with Jacksonville P. D. to investigate the claims. A number of people were interviewed, including, says Kulesa, "an Elvis impersonator, but that didn't pan out," and neither did any of the other people questioned. In fact, many of the people named in the letter had already passed away. The police however say they believe that evidence is still out there, but that the witnesses have not shown themselves.

During the original investigation, the lead investigator Frank Sturdivant, was particularly determined to solve the case. His own son had tragically died of drowning, and so for him, this became more personal. When Memphis magazine writer Marilyn Sadler went to his office to talk to him about this, she could tell he'd followed every lead, no matter how small or irrelevant they might have seemed. He was desperate to find any clues. He did admit he found himself wondering, had Matthew really drowned himself, in the bizarre pursuit of living as an Immortal Elf? But he also followed the work of the private investigator hired by Matthew's parents. This private investigator, who insisted on anonymity, found the aspects of Matthew's wet-up-to-the-knees jeans very curious and rather suspicious. The private eye also discovered some very curious information about an incident that occurred three weeks Matthew had disappeared. He discovered that on December the 28th, a trooper pulled over to check on a stationary Cadillac along the road very close to where Matthew had vanished from. The trooper noticed that the man standing beside the Cadillac appeared to be trembling uncontrollably. The trooper began to question the man and as he was doing so another man appeared, carrying a can of gasoline. The trooper thought perhaps the first man, who appeared to be the driver of the Cadillac, was shaking because he was cold. It was, afterall, the middle of the winter, and the trooper let them go on their way, but he noted down the license plate.

What the private eye discovered was that later that same day, the Cadillac returned and the driver of the Cadillac broke into a house on the same road, for the purpose it would seem, of using the telephone in the house. When the owner of the house came home carrying groceries and opened her front door, she screamed on seeing the intruder. The intruder then said very calmly to the person they were speaking to on the telephone, "I have to go. The lady of the house just came in."

Then he opened the front door and left! But as he did so, the lady whose house he had broken into noticed that in one of his hands he held a cell phone. Why then, she wondered, had he broken in to use her phone? Once she was sure he had gone, she pressed 'redial' on her phone to see what number the intruder had called. When a person answered on the other end of the line, it turned out to be a convenience store located in North Little Rock, not far from the location of her house.

The lady handed the telephone number over to the private detective, who said he ran a background check. He discovered that the worker who had answered the phone at the store had a criminal record. The driver of the Cadillac was also background checked, and in fact, the following week was arrested in Phoenix, Arizona for the possession of marijuana and mushrooms, said the detective. The Cadillac was owned by someone else – apparently a drug runner and counterfeiter who lived in Atlanta, and very strangely, only three miles from a friend of the missing student Matthew.

This friend had already been questioned by police, said the private eye, and he, as well as the police, had suspicions about this friend of Matthew, he said. The private eye also emphasized how strange a coincidence it would be that in a large city like Atlanta, this friend of Matthew's and the Cadillac driver would live in such relatively close proximity.

The detective told Memphis magazine that it went further. There had been phone calls between the Cadillac driver and Matthew's friend in Atlanta on December the 3rd. The private detective said he couldn't shake the odds that this was evidence of some kind of planned drug deal and that the missing student had perhaps been talked into helping out, and as a result had found himself there in the Bayou. The PI hypothesised that Matthew could have found himself in way-over his head, or had a change of heart about participating and panicked – by which time everyone involved panicked, and this ultimately led to murder. The private eye thinks the student's body could have been in the trunk of the Cadillac, and that they'd brought his body back to bury it in the bayou somewhere, or that his body had been hidden in the bayou and the Cadillac driver had returned to get it and bury it elsewhere. Or, did they simply just run out of gasoline? And the man was trembling because he was cold?

Strangely, Memphis Magazine, following up on this to do their own fact checking in 2008, shed doubt on the whole story. The PI was very reticent about giving any details and he was unwilling to reveal the telephone records of the supposed phone calls between the friend of the missing student and the Cadillac driver. He said this was to protect his source. The original investigator, Detective Kulesa, told Memphis Magazine however that he could find no records of such phone calls existing. The missing student's parents were more inclined to believe the private eye's story, and called him tenacious and determined. Unfortunately however, he would not give them any of the evidence in writing either, to confirm his version of what may have happened, while the police said the phone calls simply never happened.

Matthew's mother said, "They found his scent from his clothes to the water's edge in the bayou, but the mystery is that there was no scent from his clothes to his car. And it's an absolute mystery to us and to the authorities to explain that. We have no clue what could have possibly happened." Said Lieutenant James Kulesa, "It's probably one of the strangest mysteries I have ever come across since I've been in law enforcement."

Was there any correlation to the Cadillac, the house break-in and Matthew's disappearance? Did Matthew wade into the water and attempt to become an immortal elf? Who was the mentally ill man in Memphis? Who were the people in the anonymous mystery letter, if any of them were still alive? Or were these all dead ends? What did happen to Matthew Pendergrast? And where is he now?

Chapter Eleven:

The Strange Death of Edgar Allan Poe

The disappearance and demise of Edgar Allan Poe seems so eerily to have replicated the macabre and gothic stories he is so famous for. Known as the creator of the detective story and a genius for creating the growing sensations of doom and horror in his books as each page is turned, Edgar Allen Poe die almost as though he was a character in his own book; and his death is still shrouded in mystery and unanswered questions.

On September the 27th 1849, Mr. Poe vanished. He reappeared 6 days later when he was found outside a busy drinking house called Gunner's Hall in Baltimore. He was lying in the gutter in distress, his clothes in disarray. Gone was his dapper and refined attire and in their place were filthy ill-fitting clothing and scruffy, dirty shoes. His clothes looked like they no longer fitted him. When he spoke, he was incoherent. Joseph Walker, a compositor for the Baltimore Sun Newspaper happened to be passing by and he went to Poe's aid. Mr. Walker asked Poe who he could contact to come to his assistance and Poe managed to give the name of a Mr. Joseph E. Snodgrass, who was a magazine editor but also had medical training. Mr. Walker hurriedly wrote a letter to Mr. Snodgrass.

"Dear Sir, there is a gentleman rather the worse for wear, who goes by the cognomen of Edgar A. Poe, and who appears in great distress. He is in need of assistance, Yours in haste.'

When Mr. Snodgrass received the urgent summons, he ventured immediately to Baltimore. He later described Poe, rather unflatteringly, as wearing an expression of "Vacant stupidity which made me shudder. He had evidently been robbed of his clothes. So stupefied, we had to carry him out as if a corpse." He said Poe was "Unwashed, haggard, unkempt and repulsive." No-one had known Poe had gone missing for almost a week. Seven days earlier, Poe had been at home in Richmond, Virginia, with his fiancée Sarah Elmira when she had commented that he looked unwell. Upon her wishes, he had visited a friend, Jonathan Carter, who was a Doctor. Carter advised him to stay home for a few more days before making his scheduled journey to Philadelphia. However, the following day, on September the 27th, Poe left Virginia bound for Philadelphia, where he had agreed to assist a Mrs Marguerite Leon Loud in editing a collection of poems she had written. Once this was completed, Poe was scheduled to travel to New York where he would escort his aunt back to Richmond for his own wedding. No-one knew how he ended up in a gutter in Baltimore, but he would be dead within four days. "He left us with a real-life mystery," said Chris Semtner, curator of the Poe Museum. Where had Poe been in the days before he was found outside the Drinking House? The most obvious answer, given the immediate evidence, would be to say that Poe had gone on a drinking binge and now lay in the street pickled with alcohol. However, this would seem an odd thing to do for such a staunch supporter of abstinence, as Poe happened to be. Just months before his disappearance, Poe had joined the Temperance Movement, foregoing alcohol entirely, and he was a vocal member of the movement. He had been a drinker before this time, and in fact some researchers have been quick to point out that Poe was a man who could not handle his drink. One biographer of Poe, Susan Weiss describes a time in Richmond when Poe's physician had to be called to the house after Poe had fallen ill. His Doctor, she says, warned Poe that "another such attack would prove fatal," to which Poe replied, "If people would not tempt him, he would not fall!" There were those around Poe, even close friends, who seemed quite content after his death, to tarnish his reputation with allegations of too much liquor. His friend J. P. Kennedy's diary entry of October the 10th 1849 said: 'On Tuesday last, Edgar Allan Poe died in town here from the effects of a debauch. He fell in with some companion here who seduced him to the bottle. The consequence was fever, delirium and madness... A bright but unsteady light has been awfully quenched.' Kennedy however was merely going by what he had heard, not first-hand experience. Rufus Griswold, a rival to Poe, wrote a scathing obituary, although it was only discovered later that he had written it – as he had used a pseudonym. He posthumously portrayed Poe as a womaniser, drunk, and an opium addict. According to the Poe Museum, it is said that Griswold even forged many of Poe's letters after death.

Poe's friend Snodgress, who had been summoned from the gutter, went even further. Snodgress was also a member of the Temperance Movement and he began touring the country to lecture about Poe's death and the dangers of drinking.

However, says Chris Semeter at the Poe Museum, "It has been documented that after a glass of wine, he was staggering drunk. His sister had the same problem. It seemed to be hereditary." So, perhaps it wasn't so much that Poe had a drinking problem before he joined the Temperance Movement; but more that he was particularly susceptible to becoming drunk after imbibing only a very small amount of liquor? There also appears to be scientific proof, from beyond the grave, that Poe had not given into temptation and drunk himself to death. Samples of Poe's hair were taken after his death, and in more recent years they were analysed. The hair samples showed that there were low levels of lead in his body, which apparently means that this is an indication Poe had no alcohol in his body when he died, and that he had indeed remained an abstainer. This however leaves a conundrum. What else could have caused Poe's spectacular expiration? After Snodgress arrived to assist Poe, he took him to a house, but Poe's condition didn't improve and he had to be admitted to the Washington University Hospital in Baltimore. A Dr. Moran assessed Poe, and for some reason, confined him to a prison-like room with bars on the window. The doctor said Poe never regained his sensibilities and drifted in and out of delirium until he died. "He talks aloud constantly as though talking to imaginary people," the Doctor noted. When Poe was found in the street, he appeared to have lost his luggage. "He is unable to explain what has happened to him or where he has been. He appears to see imaginary objects," the Doctor said.

One theory for Poe's disappearance was that he had fallen victim to 'Cooping.' He was found outside a Drinking House that was bursting full. It was voting day in the district, and the Drinking House was the venue for the ballot boxes. In Poe's era, 'Cooping' was a popular method of voter fraud, and it was carried out as such: An unsuspecting victim would be kidnapped off the street prior to the day of the election. They would be made to change into different clothes provided by the gang who abducted them, and then they would be marched to the voting station to cast their vote for the candidate of the gang's choice. This process was then repeated multiple times, and each time the victim would be re-dressed and other attempts at disguising him, such as hats or canes would be implemented so that the victim could be marched back to the polling centre again and keep voting again and again for the same candidate. When Poe was found, he was wearing a large straw hat; something his friends and family had never seen him wear. His filthy clothes did not fit him, nor did his shoes. Dr. Moran at the hospital described his outfit as "an old bombazine coat, pantaloons of a similar character, a pair of worn-out shoes run down at the heels, and an old straw hat". He was wearing a dirty shirt but no vest.

Most usually, the 'cooping' victim would be plied with alcohol to get him to comply with their abductor's demands, yet Poe had no alcohol in him, so how did the gang, if he was kidnapped, make him do what they told him to? Did they threaten him? Beat him? Or, had he been held by them for several days somewhere, with little food and water, and perhaps little sleep? He could well have been too frightened to sleep. When he was found, was his delirium and incoherence as a result of dehydration and sleep deprivation perhaps? Would this explain his condition? But then why would he go on to die, once he was treated in the hospital? Dr. Moran said Poe drifted in and out of delirium until he died.

Another theory presented in 1999 at the International Edgar Allan Poe Conference, was offered by public health researcher Albert Donnay. He said that Poe's death was as a result of carbon monoxide poisoning from coal gas used for lighting lamps in houses in 19th century. Although Donnay also used hair samples taken from Poe after death, donated to him by the Edgar Allan Poe Society of Baltimore, which he tested for heavy metals, the results for carbon monoxide were 'inconclusive.' There was however higher than normal levels of mercury. One possible reason for this could be because of Poe's exposure to an epidemic of cholera in the 1840's. Poe had been prescribed medicine which contained traces of mercury to treat it. The symptoms of mercury poisoning can include delirium and hallucinations. However, the levels of mercury found in Poe were many times lower than the level required for it to be poisonous.

Dr. Moran at the hospital said Poe talked continuously. "On repeated occasions, Poe was observed to be calling out for someone. The person's name he called was "Reynolds." No-one could find out who this person was. When Dr. Moran tried to reassure Poe that his friend "Reynolds" would soon come, Poe's reply was cryptic indeed. He said, "The best thing he could do would be to blow out his brains with a pistol." Why would Poe say this? And who was Reynolds?

Poe died in his hospital room on October the 7th. His final words according to Dr. Moran were, "Lord help my poor soul." What he actually died of has never been solved. Most mysteriously, Poe's medical notes have never been found. Why did he die? And who was this "Reynolds"?

One possible Reynolds was found in a bankruptcy petition written by Poe in 1842. Another Reynolds was a carpenter who happened to be serving at the Polls as an Election Judge. His name was Henry R. Reynolds, but it is not known if Poe knew him at all. Biographer Arthur Hobson Quinn wonders if Poe was referring to Jeremiah Reynolds, lecturer and explorer and 'projector of the voyages to the South Seas, whose very language Poe had used in his short story Message found in a bottle.' This Reynolds propounded the Hollow Earth Theory; that Earth's interior was hollow and habitable and accessible via openings at the North and South poles. But why did Poe say, whichever Reynolds he was referring to, that he would be better to blow his brains out? Where was Poe for 6 days before he died? And what caused his death?

Chapter Twelve:

Who was The Dolocher?

We travel back in time now to Georgian times, and in Dublin, Ireland, a Beast was stalking the streets of the city, rendering terror into the hearts of its inhabitants, and not everyone escaped its claws. The saga began inside the Black Dog of Dublin, which was a Prison located in Browne's Castle, in Newhall Market. From the early 18th century, the Black Dog operated as a prison both for common criminals and for debtors, and the length of sentence to be served by each prisoner was not determined by a magistrate but by their creditor. The prison was operated privately, and prisoners could rent their bed for the price of a shilling-a-night. For the many prisoners who could not afford to pay this sum of money, they were consigned to a damp and tiny, claustrophobic dungeon with very little air. The only light in this dungeon came in through a sewer which ran beside the dungeon. The terrible air quality and the feted stench, was said to have been unbearable. It was at this prison that a man called 'Dolocher' was kept, after the 'Violation of female purity, accorded by murder,' wrote the Dublin Penny Journal in 1832. He had murdered a young local girl. Dolocher was kept in this to be hanged for his crime.

However, just before his death sentence was due to be carried out, he killed himself. The spirit of this prisoner did not leave the prison. It lingered willingly, wanting to reap its vengeance. It haunted this jail, in the form of a terrifying beast, and this beast was believed to be behind a number of very grisly and unexplained deaths.

It began a few nights after the prisoner's suicide, when one of the sentries, whose duty it was to guard the condemned prisoners' cells, including Olocher's old cell, was found insensible and paralyzed, seemingly with terror or shock, and he was discovered lying at the bottom of a flight of stairs which led out to the street. The sentry had strange injuries to his body. He looked as though he had been mauled by a wild animal. His clothes were distressed and torn. They looked as though they had been ripped apart by claws of some kind.

Later, when the sentry finally recovered sufficiently to speak, he explained that he had heard noises coming out of Olocher's now empty cell. Confused by this, the sentry had walked towards the cell to investigate. As he opened Olocher's dark cell, something that defied his mind came flying out at him. The sentry declared that he had been attacked by a half-man, half-beast and it was a devil, he said. Though he had recovered well enough to speak, one side of his body was still powerless, as if he had been struck by a paralytic stroke, caused, it was assumed, by the sight of this beast, which he declared had appeared in the form of a half-human black pig.

The next night, a sentry alerted the head guard that he too had seen the Devil, in the form of a half-man, half-beast. For several nights in a row, the guards continued to report seeing this terrifying creature. 'For several nights the guards were regularly called out, who all declared that they had seen this strangely fearful and unnatural appearance,' said the Penny Journal.

Soon, the residents of Dublin would be warning each other not to walk alone down dark alleys at night, for fear that they too would become victim to the Demon known now as 'The Olocher.' That winter, fear gripped the residents. They were all terrified that they would come face to face with this half-human demon with the head of a pig.

A week after the first attack at the Black Dog Prison, another sentry was puzzled to find that the guard he had come to relieve from duty, was not at his station. The sentry had disappeared. All that remained of him was his rifle leaning against the wall, and his uniform which had been draped over the rifle as though to appear in the shape of a human body. What trickery was this? Where was the guard?

'He had been devoured!' reported the Penny Journal, 'When the relief went around about 12 o'clock, he could not be found. Looking behind the sentry box, they perceived the figure of a man – but on closer inspection, it was found to be the fated victim's gun dressed up with his clothes, even to his shirt and fully accounted.

Consternation and terror spread on every side. The most sensible people of the day were of the opinion that Olocher had taken the shape of a Black pig and had left the mark of his infernal vengeance on the first sentry, and had carried off this last one body and soul!'

Then the attacks outside of the prison. 'The next day, a woman came before the Magistrates and made oath that she saw the Dolocher, by which name it ever afterwards went, in Christ Church Lane. That it made a bite at her, held fast her cloak with its tusks, and that through fright she fled and left it with the monster.'

The attacks were escalating. Night after night the alarm would be raised. 'It was now shrewdly whispered about, that as the wretched Olocher was to suffer death for a particular crime, his hatred to women tormented him after his suicide, and that he roved the earth to annoy them; for the assaults of the monster were particularly directed against the fairer sex. The demon reigned triumphant.'

A vigilante group formed together in an attempt to find the 'Pig-Man' and kill it. 'A set of brave resolute fellows banded together to rid the city of such a tormentor.' Drinkers in one of the pubs in Cook Street also set out as a posse to kill any black pigs they could find running through the streets of Dublin. 'They sallied out one night from a pub, armed with clubs, rusty swords, knives, determined to slay every black pig they met. The slaughter commenced – such as breaking of legs, fracturing of skulls, maiming and destroying.' Why would pigs be running through the streets of Dublin? - Well in those days, Dublin was a wild concoction of vibrant life, which included the free-reign of animals. Writer Caroline Barry describes the rich and evocative streets she discovered when researching for her novel set in those time. 'Georgian Dublin was exciting, violent, wild and densely populated with rogues and vagabonds, thieves and jilts, and ordinary decent folk. The rich and the poor lived cheek by jowl. The streets were narrow, hopping with preachers, eccentrics. There were periwig makers. Bears were kept at the back of wig shops to be slaughtered for their grease. There were coffee shops where exotic animals were fed scraps. There were jelly houses frequented by transvestites, molly houses visited by homosexuals, in the taverns were clubs of every kind, lottery shops painted gaudy colors, lit with mirrors and chandeliers.' "Hell" was an infamous district in the center of Dublin, notorious for rebel-rousers, and 'crammed with brothels. Dog baiting, cock fighting and bare-knuckle boxing took place there.'

So, from the Pub in the heart of 'Hell', the pig-posse set out, slaughtering any pig they came across with violence and vengeance, hoping one of them would be 'The Olocher.' Reported in the Penny Journal, 'When any old pig would be difficult to kill, the women in the houses would shiver and exclaim, "Oh! They have him now! Them are the boys …the Devil's cure to the Beast!" and such like. Yet all the while, neither man, woman or child dare put their heads outside the doors to assist them.' Perhaps they were successful; for 'No Dolocher appeared again that winter.' However, 'Next winter, the Dolocher reappeared again.' A young woman passing by Fisher's alley was pulled in. The alarm spread again,' and the Dolocher recommenced his 'Reign of terror.' 'Even the hearts of men trembled within them at thought of encountering so dreadful a combatant.'

One day, a local woman claimed the 'Pig-Man' had attacked her as she walked alone in Christ Church Lane. She was pregnant and she claimed the beast had caused her to lose the baby. Then, 'One day, a blacksmith came into Dublin on business. He was described as 'a brawny fellow with a heart as hard and impervious to fear as his fist was as a sledge-hammer.' After the blacksmith had finished with his appointments, had been completed, he went to a Tavern where he spent a few hours drinking with his friends. As night fell, he realized he should begin making the several-mile journey back home. The rain was descending in torrents and so he wrapped himself up in a coat belonging to his friend's wife. 'Just as the blacksmith reached Hell,' out rushed The Dolocher, 'Who pounced on its victim and pinned him against the wall. The Blacksmith was not a man to die easy, and he raised his muscular arm, "Be you Dolocher or the Devil, take that!" letting a thumper fall. Down dropped the Dolocher. The valiant Blacksmith shouted, "I've killed the Dolocher!" A crowd cautiously collected. The dying groaning devil was lifted up, and out of a black pig's skin came the very man who had been carried off body and soul from his post at the Black Dog! The Dolocher was removed to the hospital, where he died the next day; but before death he confessed, that by his assistance, the prisoner Olocher had committed suicide, and a low female spread the first report of the Black Pig - and he had thus kept up the delusion for the purpose of robbery.'

The riddle of the preternatural pig had finally been solved. The missing sentry, wearing a pig's head and pig's skin, had transformed himself into the beast The Olocher, to rob the good people of Dublin through means of preternatural terror, but the blacksmith had finally brought down his reign and unmasked him!

Chapter Thirteen:

The MAY DAY Mystery

Mr. Robert Hungerford, lawyer, a member of Mensa, and a graduate of the University of Arizona has for the last few decades taken out an Advert in the University of Arizona's Wild Cat Newspaper, on behalf, he says, of an 'Organisation' that he legally represents. He is unable to give any details about this mystery organisation, other than that they have a mission of sorts; though the mission is unknown and has remained so since at least the early eighties. The adverts in the Wild Cat, which invariably appear around May the first each year, though sometimes there are bonus adverts at other times, has lent the Organisation and its cryptic puzzles to being called 'The May Day Mystery.' A former Student at the University of Arizona, Brian Hance, noticed the adverts in the Wild Cat, and when he took a position working for the college newspaper, his curiosity increased to the point that he collected all the adverts and placed them on a website. Some people who stumbled across this website became intrigued by the ads too, and they began sending in possible solutions to some of the many complex features of the ads -

which are often comprised of infinitely intricate geometric patterns, highly complex mathematical and physics formulae, dates, co-ordinates, archaic quotes from religion, philosophy,

history and literature. There are messages in the adverts too, often written in a number of foreign languages, from Chinese to Hebrew to Arabic, and sometimes there are musical compositions. Strange phrases appear and also statements that seem to be talking about upcoming meetings for the Organisation's members. The Organisation appears to have some kind of strata to it, and Mr. Hance would soon begin to be contacted by the Organisation. There is the Orphanage, who often communicate directly with Mr. Hance by email or post, or they give messages to 'The Order of the Un-reconstructed Freaks' to contact Mr. Hance on their behalf. Then there are the Heirlings, who seem to be at the beck and call of The Orphanage members and often appear to be 'in transit,' if this interpretation is correct. 'The Orphanage has reserved the Haussdorff room of the Hotel California,' says one advert, and most times, their meetings are at this Hotel, though where it is physically located many have tried to work out.

The May Day Ad of 2004 includes, 'Child: continue to use the local yokel pigs as an (easily) accessible platform and electrical conduit – who will remain a mouldering menagerie of middle-aged meat-puppets until they are consumed at das Schlachtfest.' Who are these 'pig' people? And what on earth do The Orphanage mean by this?

One email sent directly to Mr. Hance in November 2008 from a 'Jenny Geddes,' claiming to be under the instruction of The Orphanage, signs off with, 'May we meet you at the right hand of the Father.' In the bible, Jesus stood at the right hand of God. The same message begins cryptically with, 'Greetings Mr. Hance, we haven't met but you have probably seen me. Not as I really am, a true, Oath-bound Freak but instead a well-turned chickie spouting nonsense on the screen which serves as the standard, officially accepted heroin for millions of the masses. What I actually do is travel and deliver messages under direct instructions from The Orphanage. I belong to what might be termed the second generation of this axial movement--although we really "date" from before the Creation when God the Father chose the Elect.' The sender seems to be saying she works on tv, as a reporter or presenter, and yet there is the esoteric implication that 'they' are as ancient as time. In 1998, one email received by Hance told him, 'On June 25th he might go in the great hall and not see anybody even though Plenary Session was in full swing and everybody present, he'd think the place was empty and silent for centuries.' It is as though the members of this organization are not of this physical earth. And yet, so many references are made to physical meetings; the May 2001 ad says, 'The loyal order of the Unreconstructed Freaks will treat us to porcine extispicy; in light of which de Moivre has suggested that one course consist of boudin ant-llais.' One 'de Moivre' was a French mathematician of the 1700's famous for a formula that links complex numbers and trigonometry. Boudin ant-llais is pork sausage. There are also often strange references to 'experiments.' The same advert says, 'As for the ongoing somatic experiment, it would now be wiser for The Asylum Choir to follow standard pharmaceutical regimes (eg abinitio; cyclosporine.) If the subject survives and becomes hemodynamically stable and asymptomatic, do not be misled by the reduction in the QRS voltage.' Sleep experiments? Brain experiments? It sounds like a club for Frankenstein afficionados; for re-animation or building human robots or something! In 2003, Tucson Weekly interviewed Mr. Hungerford about his Organisation, to which he responded, "It is in all likelihood that I am a disturbed, mentally ill person, and these writings are no doubt the ravings of a madman." The magazine called him 'A self-described anti-social hermit.' He said, "It is entirely possible that all of this is the work of one person, disturbed or otherwise. It could be for amusement, could be mental illness, could be anything," although he then adds, "But, on the other hand, that wouldn't be a bad cover, if one needed a cover." 'His downtown office is littered with books on cryptography, languages, history, medicine, physics. While he possesses a vast collection of language-to-language dictionaries, almanacs, encyclopaedias, all the perfect resources to design the group's most complex cypher adverts, Hungerford denies he has ever read the volumes in his office, "I pick out books because of their colour, nothing more," he quips to the Magazine. 'Between an assortment of machetes, knives and guns on his walls are handwritten messages in Hebrew, hieroglyphics,' along with stamp collections and pictures of anatomy. It would seem that Mr. Hungerford would be the perfect person to be behind the creation of the ads all by himself, without there being any secret society, yet over the years Mr. Hance has been sent stamps from remote countries far and wide, so who is sounding those? Mr. Hungerford's registered office in downtown Tucson is around the corner from the Scottish Rite Freemason's building. Hungerford seems to imply in his very infrequent interviews that the Organization he has also called 'The Brotherhood,' are not opposed to attracting new members. "Like a tuning fork there is resonance with the right people," he said. A message sent to Brain Hance reads, "The day you can see the door, you will be welcomed inside." Are Hungerford and the Scottish Rite of Freemasons in cahoots? Is this simply a recruiting method for the local Freemasons? 'The Orphanage' calls to mind the phrase 'The widow's son' in Freemasonry, with the 'son' being the central character of an allegory presented to all candidates during the third degree in Freemasonry; yet wouldn't that be too simple as an obvious answer? Who's sending the stamps, postcards and letters from remote African villages or the Far East, for example? A letter received from The Orphanage by Brian Hance in 2000 points out, 'While much data can be gleaned by considering "secret orders," you are not dealing with Rosicrucian's or Freemasons. Learn what you can from any source but do not pigeonhole.' They also point out, to those who have said they must be the 'illuminati;' 'Greetings from The Orphanage. If such phrase appears in your postings, it was not from The Orphanage. The (alleged) "Illuminati" are indeed inoffensive and ineffective. Foolish people wearing silly hats and clothes that don't fit. We are interested in fundamental CHANGE and that necessarily incorporates Death rather than external trivialities." This could be seen as rather sinister, given the mentioning of death being necessary, yet again, doesn't it seem to be more of an esoteric meaning, of life-after-death and the continuation of the soul?

Brian Hance says he can't pinpoint who is behind the messages, though he admitted to Tucson Weekly in 2003 that he has met Robert Hungerford at his office, when he apparently went there to fix his computer. Is Hance also part of the game? Could he even be writing these communications to himself? However, he claims to be just as puzzled by it all. "There's the lone gunman theory," he says, "which I've discarded as too long-running, complex and expensive." If the ads have been running since the early eighties, that would bring the bill to at least $40,000 so far. When Phoenix Mag spoke to Robert Hungerford, he told them, "The May Day mystery arose out of a group formed in August 1969. There were earlier messages than the first in 1981, but they were in a different medium." Why do they use a University newspaper, with such a limited audience? One would think they would be looking for far more attention, but perhaps not. Along with philosophical and theological messages and quotations, there are other messages that could be taken to be quite sinister too, unless of course it's all simply gibberish. One message received by Mr. Hance, for example, is highly strange. It came from one of the 'Unreconstructed Freaks,' and said (translated from what looks like a form of Afrikaans or Jamaican slang!) 'Ever wonder how we're doing this? Having visions of Fort Detrick and MK Ultra?' Well, although 'MK Ultra' may sound like a crazy sci-fi conspiracy, Martin Cannon wrote 'The Controllers' in 1990, and in this he claims to have read over 200,000 pages of documents from organizations including the CIA and the Department of Defense, as well as statements and witness testimonies, and from this Cannon believed he had found that a person's mind could be controlled, to the point for example, that they could believe they'd had an encounter with alien entities. "The kidnapping is real; the fear is real. The pain is real. But little grey men from Zeti Reticuli are not real; they are constructs; Halloween masks to disguise the real faces... Evidence exists," he says, "linking members of the Intel community; CIA, Naval Intelligence, DARPA, with esoteric technology of mind control... For decades, 'spychiatrists' have been working behind the scenes - on college campuses. They have experimented with the erasing of memory, hypnotic resistance to torture, hypnotic suggestion, microwave induction of "voices," and a host of even more disturbing tech." What's more, when 'MK Ultra' was uncovered, there were 149 sub-projects operating on College Campuses. Is it still going on? Yes, according to Martin Cannon. Could the people behind The Orphanage be some kind of secret government black ops project? But surely, that's too preposterous for words, isn't it? Or is this some kind of black magic stemming from the medieval ages, when it was called necromancy or sorcery, or the more contemporary chaos magic? Some have said that their Adverts look encrypted with magical sigils.

The email message to Hance from 'The Freaks' says of MK Ultra, 'Lot of that going on for sure but no news there. There are other ways that the dumb ain't pursuing... Don't need no knock on door, don't need no disguise, kick it in, rip the fat off their bones, write helter-skelter on the wall with their worthless blood and then roll back to the truck and head south of the line. Keystone Cops go nuts looking for the last of Charlie Manson's people.' Counter-culture villain Charles Manson's followers slaughtered a movie director's wife, Sharon Tate in 1969, and wrote in blood on the walls, "PIGS." They wanted a social revolution, and as Hungerford has pointed out in interviews, the May Day Organisation is aiming for 'Revolution' of sorts too, although presumably, not quite in so literal a sense!

One advert has a quote from Sampson, 'Thus, those he killed at death were more than he had slain in his life,' but again, this is a religious reference, not one of literal violence. The May Day Advert in 2019 ends with the quote, 'I was shaken with love and dread.' This is a quote from Augustine of Hippo 354 – 430 AD, who was a Catholic Bishop, and its about God. An ad in 1999 says, 'The art of conversing with stones is called physics, JT Fraser,' followed by B= Triangulate,' and other phrases, including 'A wink is as good as a nod to a blind horse'! while the 2008 May Day ad includes, 'Mistah Kurtz will present our new line of jams and jellies!' and is surrounded by formulae and equations. One May Day advert has as its top line; 'These are not natural events; They strengthen from strange to stranger,' W.S.' This is a quote from William Shakespeare; but if anyone were to believe the meaning of the many quotes and references are easy to decipher and interpret, because they recognize a quote or two, then they would be quickly fooled. This particular advert ends with 'Mistah Kurtz is instructed to supress the infestation of Taenia solium – the specific ontological taeniasis has been traced by Ireton to the Pelagian devils.' Followed by this is The Orphanage's signature smiley-face. Taenia solium is pork tapeworm. Kurtz was the central character in Joseph Conrad's Heart of Darkness, a figure who transforms into a despot and mini god in the jungle. There is also a reference to Conrad's Kurtz in the writing of T.S Elliot. Yet the reason for this reference, if indeed it is referring to Conrad's fictional character, is unexplained. For the vast majority of references, quotes, notes, and phrases, in whatever language they are presented in the ads, do not make for easy understanding in the context of the adverts, given that they are comprised of a multitude of seemingly unrelated links, formulae, equations et al. The May 1st 1994 advert, for example, has predominately numbers, symbols, and formula. One could imagine the Organisation is an elite club for genius intellectuals who enjoy games of extremely difficult puzzle-solving, or, it could simply be a member's dining club! – there is the mention of Hors d'oeuvre in some adverts! Could it all simply be a sophisticated 'in - joke'.

A recurring theme among the adverts is the reference to 'Pelagian devils,' Augustine, and Luther. In an email communication to Mr. Hance from two characters calling themselves 'Rocky and Bullwinkle,' they say, 'The Pelagian devils are close behind us. Thanks to the grace of the Triune God--He who alone is both One and yet Three, the same known to Moses and to Our Lord Jesus.' In one message, the 'Freak' tells Hance. 'The Orphanage and Dallas Section send their regards. 50 years and the Pelagian devils have not been able to replace The Usurper.' Another message includes, 'Celebrate the exposure of the Pelagian devils as perverts and sodomites.' Pelagius (c. AD 354 – 418) was a British monk who believed there was no original sin and that moral decisions could be made through people's free will without the need for divine intervention. He advocated free will and asceticism. Augustine brought the Reformation. Augustine accused Pelagius for teaching that moral perfection was attainable in life through human free will without divine grace. Augustine contradicted this by saying perfection was impossible without grace because we are born sinners with a sinful heart and will. There seems to be an underlying theme in the May Day adverts and communications, that God and Man are sovereign in a synergistic relationship, where man has free will but can only be saved through accepting Jesus, and man must work in faith to Jesus to ensure his eternal life, although I could have got this wrong. There is also much mention of Luther, (1483–1546), an Augustinian monk who rejected teachings of the Catholic Church. He challenged the authority of the Pope by teaching that the Bible is the only source of divine knowledge. Luther taught that salvation leading to man's eternal life are not earned through the action of good deeds but are received as the gift of God's grace through belief in Jesus as our redeemer of sins. He believed in the continuity of a person's identity beyond death. Lutherans believe a person is saved by God's grace through faith in Christ alone. When it comes to salvation, all that matters is faith in Jesus, and unlike the Roman Catholic Church, Lutherans do not believe the office of the papacy as such has any divine authority. This is the most simplistic view, and not being a Theologian myself, there may be many errors and misinterpretations in this, and certainly, this simplistic explanation would not meet the expectations of The Orphanage, who from their messages and sophisticated adverts are certainly highly knowledgeable and learned in scholarly religion, as well as many other disciplines. It is impossible to do their knowledge justice, and really, study of theology would be essential to understand the Orphanage's religious messages and meanings and beliefs.

May 1st was when the illuminati in Bavaria was formed. May 1st is also supposedly. April 30th. This is Walpurgisnacht, or 'Walpurgis Night' – the night of the Witch, sometimes also called Beltane, but most commonly known as May Day. We may picture the innocent custom of dancing round Maypoles, but the ancient Druids would sacrifice a human at this time, to appease the gods and hope for good harvest, like in the ghastly film 'The Wicker Man' where the victim is placed on a huge pile of wood and burnt in a bonfire. These days however, we have a straw effigy instead of a human being; the burning man. On Walpurgisnacht in ancient Germanic folklore, a Harlequin figure leads an army of ghosts and lost souls. The harlequin is the leader of the involuntary dead.

One person attempting to help solve the mystery of the organisation found this; 'So, I'm reading through the Mass. Lawyers Weekly and boom here's this quarter-page ad with a weird seal at the top titled 'Knights of Thermopylae Inn of Court.' The advert says, 'Law Day, May 1, is a special day in the United States, a day when the secular priests and worshippers of America's new religion the Law take time to go public to spread the faith requiring the Brahmin Dorian Gray's of the Bar take time to assure there is still an appropriate cover on their portraits, the wealthy members of the Plaintiff's Bar to stop circling for the best carrion and other such sacrifices by the power-that-be.' The people behind this advert point out that the rest of the world celebrate International Workers Day on May 1, and that in America this day included the event of the Haymarket Riots in 1886 in Chicago over worker's rights; an event which led to several men being hung and this organisation, the Knights of Thermopylae Inn of Court, believes wrongly, and that they were killed for challenging law, power and the wealthy. Is this related to the May Day Mystery?

"Someone is spending an inordinate amount of time and money on this thing," said Hance once. The cost of an Advert in the section of the newspaper in the eighties is estimated at around $1,000. "At first, I believed it was an individual with a lot of both to spare, then my theory moved to a group of friends playing a game. Now, I have run out of theories..." Hance continues to receive packages that come from around the world. Are members of The Orphanage frequent travellers? Or do they have members in many countries? Mr. Hungerford appears to be on the board of directors for a non-profit organisation registered to his office, which helps people in the Congo by obtaining and shipping medicine to them. Perhaps he travels far and wide? But Mr. Hance has received phone calls too, from a number of different voices including females. Are these Mr Hungerford's friends? Their identities are never given when they leave a message. Yet Hungerford is an eccentric recluse, supposedly. Does he pay people to phone Mr. Hance? Is it all just an elaborate prank? A frat game that has continued for decades now? Or a discordian game? Is it intellectual jiggery and meaningless nonsense? 'Worthy of Sherlock Holmes for its perplexing weirdness, is a perennial headscratcher in Tucson that has stumped residents with a 35-year trail of bizarre clues,' said Phoenix Mag in 2017. Mr. Hance said, "I'm surprised the postal service has not put me on the 'watch list' given the wild things they've held for me." The parcels and packages come from countries including Pakistan, and often contain postcards, old stamps or rare coins. Theories come and go. Hance said that of the many who have tried to solve the puzzle, one person insisted on meeting Hance in person to tell him that this was the work of the (un-caught) Zodiac Killer. "That made for an entertaining evening," said Hance, "but it was not the last. Sometimes I wish they'd never contacted me at all." He means The Organisation. "My involvement in the mystery went from simple to far too complex with one email. I wonder what they'd do to me if I just stopped."

Thomas Bradwardine for the Orphanage contacted Mr. Hance on one occasion. 'Greetings, Mr. Hance; this is not a sub-plenary but rather we received word at this location, to remind you that today is St. Michael and All Angels' Day. Remember the context in which he is famous -- it was not for standing for one of your elections. We could care less whom is "elected" -- a tool is a tool. The point of writing, as explained to us at this location by The Orphanage, is to make clear not only the combative nature of this undertaking -- hence the commemoration of this day -- but also that the King of the Universe has His agents spread throughout creation, including places, such as this one, which are useful but unexpected. Grace and peace, Thomas Bradwardine for the Orphanage."

'Endecott' of The Orphanage writes cryptically to Hance, 'The Hirelings are watchful. You are in no danger but others are. Small thing to lose this difficult life when feasting at the right hand of the Father is assured. Grace and peace. Endecott.' What is the mission of The Orphanage?

It is known that often those who journey down the rabbit hole of the May Day Mystery will become the recipient of some unusual mail, so be warned… The Orphanage have a habit of contacting those who dive into their mystery….

Chapter Fourteen:

Who was the mysterious Showman?

In 1885, a young girl arrived to live on a rural farm in Shawville, Pontiac County, Quebec. She had been adopted by the family who lived there, farmer Mr. George Dagg and his wife Susan, who lived on the farm with their children. The farm itself was located a few miles north of the Ottawa river and it was set among a rich and vast forest of pine trees. The Dagg family had emigrated from Ireland and they now lived in this farmhouse, which was actually just a wood cabin comprising of three rooms. The family had two daughters, Mary aged five, and Eliza Jane four, and an eighteen-month old son called Johnny. There was also a young orphan boy called Dean who helped at the farm doing chores. Mr. Dagg's parents lived a couple of miles away.

In 1885, Mr. and Mrs Dagg had adopted the 9-year-old girl from a placement home in nearby Belleville. Her name was Dina Burden McLean. It seemed that she settled in very well with her new family, and according to all accounts, she was treated very well by them and was considered to be as much a part of the family as Mr and Mrs Dagg's biological children. There are certainly no reports of any problems, and Dina wrote to her own mother to say she was happy there. Four years later however, the circumstances were to unexpectedly and dramatically change for the worse. One day, while Mr Dagg was out working on the farm, Mrs Dagg returned home from running some errands to find a trail of excrement lining the floor of their wooden home. It seems that the mother and father, for some reason, believed this had been done by their farm hand, the young orphan boy. In fact, they would take him before a magistrate to deal with him and have him answer for his actions.

This however did not resolve the issue, after similar incidents happened again. Excrement continued to be found, thrown around the house but the magistrate did not find any grounds for blaming the orphan boy and he was exonerated. He was very upset to be accused however, and he left the farm, never to return. Mr. and Mrs. Dagg expected this to be the end of the matter, but really, this was just the beginning. One day, shortly after the boy left, the family were all inside their cabin when one of the glass windows suddenly, violently shattered inwards. Naturally, the father immediately believed someone had thrown a rock at their window from outside, and he ran out to apprehend them, but he found no-one there. Rather than returning back inside, Mr. Dagg decided to hide outside behind a barn, where he waited expectantly for the hooligan to return.

Instead, he watched in horror as another glass window shattered; yet no person was there to have caused it to shatter. On another occasion, one of the children was hit hard on the head when a large stone appeared to be thrown by an invisible hand through the open door of the cabin. Even more alarmingly, soon there would be arson. A total of eight separate fires broke out inside the wood cabin, causing much distress, fear and panic to all. Again, no-one was ever seen setting a fire. Then the attacks began to get more serious. Dina, the adopted daughter, seemed to be targeted the most. She would suddenly experience her hair being sharply pulled. She would shriek out in pain, causing the rest of the family to run to where she was, only to find great chunks of her hair gone from her head. But if they were to think that she was perhaps doing this to herself; the same thing happened to their son too, and very oddly, most of his hair would soon look like it had been shorn unevenly-off his head!

One day, as Dina was helping her mother with bedroom chores, she screeched: "Look! Look! The big black thing is pulling off the bedclothes!!" Mary, her sister, urged Dina to pick up the nearby whip and beat it, and this Dina did do – which resulted in the big black thing making a sound like a squealing pig and vanishing before their eyes. Then a mouth organ which was lying on a shelf suddenly raised up into the air and began playing a tune, before being hurled violently across the room.

An armchair began to rock back and forth, manically. A wooden moto which hung upon the wall was torn from its place and seen thumping the bed several times. Potatoes became the black thing's weapon of choice, and each member of the family would regularly find themselves being struck hard by a flying potato. It was not long after this that Mary saw something else just as horrifying as the black thing. She saw something that appeared to her in the shape of a man, but it had horns on its head and cloven hooves instead of feet. It was standing silently in the doorway of her bedroom. It reappeared to her again sometime later, but this time it was dressed all in white. The figure asked her; "Do you want to go to Hell with me?" Dina encountered this strange man too. Sometimes, he seemed capable of appearing in the form of a huge black dog with "long black hair and tails." The man seemed to be able to appear in many forms, including a tall man with a cow's head.

Word soon spread locally of the peculiar occurrences at the Dagg farm. The Ottawa Free Press reported, 'A Clarendon Spirit tells who he is. The enterprise shown in despatching a reporter to personally enquire into the strange proceedings has attracted general attention and a rush of curiosity seekers to investigate.'

A Reverend Horner arrived, keen to lead the family in spiritual prayer. He gathered the family together and held a group prayer session in the cabin. He began to read aloud from the Bible, but the Bible was wrestled from his hands and completely vanished into thin air in front of everyone. Later, the bible was discovered inside the oven in the kitchen.

Young Dina told Mr. and Mrs. Dagg that she had begun to hear a deep gruff voice talking to her. She said the voice would follow her around. She said the language it used was vile and obscene. Then the rest of the family began to hear it too.

With the neighbourhood and indeed much of the county and further afield hearing about the strange and sinister happenings, soon everyone wanted to go there to see it for themselves. Newspapers far and wide began to report on the mystifying phenomena occurring at the farm. Witnesses attested to the local newspaper, 'When Dina is present, a deep gruff voice liking that of an aged man has been heard both in the house and outdoors, and when asked questions, answered so as to be distinctly heard, showing that he is cognizant of all that has taken place.'

One curious visitor to the Dagg's home was a Mr. Percy Woodcock. He was an artist and a reporter for the Brockville Recorder and Times, and he wished to investigate what was happening. 'Many laughed, leaving it to Woodcock to liaise between spirit and man.'

Mr. Woodcock took Dina aside and asked her; had she heard the strange voice today? She replied that she had heard it only a few moments earlier, when she had been outside near one of the farm sheds. Mr. Woodcock asked her to show him where this was and she accompanied him to it. No sooner had they arrived at the woodshed than Mr. Woodcock was addressed personally by the invisible man. "I am the Devil. I will have you in my clutches. Get out of this or I'll break your neck!"

The researcher was stunned and rooted to the spot in apprehension momentarily, until he found his own voice.

Bravely, he chastised this invisible man for such threats. However, the response he received in reply was yet more threatening. Dina told Mr. Woodcock about the odd message she had found scrawled on one of the walls in recent days. "You gave me fifteen cuts," it said. What did this message mean? Were "cuts" like lashes of the whip?

Mr. Woodcock came up with the idea of producing a pencil and a piece of paper and inviting the 'man' to write on it, in an effort to get him to communicate more with them. According to both Mr. Woodcock and Dina, after placing the piece of paper and pencil down, the pencil was lifted into the air a few moments later by an unseen hand. The message it wrote, as perhaps by now should have been expected, was full of more threats of violence to come. Mr. Woodcock, in an attempt to rule out the possibility that Dina could somehow be doing all of these tricks herself, filled her mouth with water so that she would not be able to talk and "throw" her voice, like a ventriloquist. Quickly came the deep gruff voice once more, and it became apparent that Dina could not be doing this with a closed mouth full of water. The conversation between Mr. Woodcock and the invisible man, it was said, then continued for some hours, until Mr. Woodcock was utterly exhausted. Said the Ottawa Citizen newspaper, 'Mr. Woodcock engaged the spirit in an epic debate, according to Greg Graham, a local historian. "They began debating philosophy, theology, the nature of God, right and wrong. When he made the ghost mad, Dina would react as if she was slapped, kicked, hit and punched. It got very violent against Dina and he'd have to back off!"

In 1889, The Ottawa Free Press reported, 'That gentleman's adventures are little else than marvellous and the sworn testimony he exhibits seems to prove satisfactorily that there actually exists airy spirits beyond the ken of mortal eye. Mr. Woodcock declined to be scared. The Spirit called him opprobrious names. Mr Woodcock took the position that he had to deal with an individual personality as real as though there in the flesh, and on this basis endeavouring to shame him into better behaviour, the voice finally admitted that it had been actuated solely by the spirit of mischief, of having fun, as it termed it, and had no ill will against anybody except Woodcock and Dina,' which was rather unfortunate for both of them!

Meanwhile, Dina's adoptive father Mr. Dagg was looking for his own solution to the family's torment. He had gone to visit a local woman called Mrs Elizabeth Barnes. She had the reputation for being a 'seer', one who possessed the ability of 'second sight.' Mrs. Barnes was more commonly known as 'The Witch of Plum Hollow,' according to the nickname locals had given her. Mrs. Barnes told Mr. Dagg that the reason for this malevolent intruder was because of the actions of a person who lived locally. Mrs. Barnes told him that "The black arts" were being used against his family. She said that a woman, a boy, and a girl who lived close-by were using dark magic against him and his family. Mr. Dagg's mind instantly turned to a Mrs. Wallace, a widow with a young daughter and a young son. Mr. Dagg was currently embroiled in an ongoing boundary dispute over some ancient land with Mrs. Barnes.

When Mr. Dagg returned to the farm, he told Mr. Woodcock of what Mrs. Barnes had told him. Mr. Woodcock decided to question the invisible man about this, and the voice told him instantly that Mrs. Wallace had indeed sent him to persecute the Dagg family on her behalf. Mr. Woodcock asked the voice when this would stop, to which the voice replied, "You meddle. I won't tell you. Shut up. I will break your neck for I am the Devil, the son of the blessed." The voice added that this was all just "Fun" to him; that he enjoyed it.

The researcher Woodcock decided that he must go to the accused woman and ask her if she really had been casting black magic against the Dagg family. That very evening, Woodcock went to Mrs. Warren's home and asked her outright. He even convinced her to go with him back to the Dagg's home. She protested all innocence in being involved in any such a thing. As soon as she arrived at the cabin, the sinister voice rang out for all to hear. It informed everyone in the room that this woman had used a book of magic and that after using it she had hidden it in the swamp. The astonished Mrs. Wallace, according to the Philadelphia Inquirer of January the 13th 1890, 'Declared she knew nothing about it and came over to the house to show she was possessed of no grudge.' After holding court for some time, the voice then said it was going to leave now. It said it would return tomorrow evening to say its final goodbye.

When the next evening arrived, a crowd came to the farm for the final chance to hear the voice. Very strangely however, now it claimed to be an Angel. Its voice was now sweet as honey. "I am sent from Heaven, sent by God. Sent to drive that fellow away." Some in the crowd, particularly Mr. Woodcock, were not so sure. One of the men gathered there asked the voice to tell everyone about something only this man knew; a secret he had shared with no-one. The voice spoke aloud, instantly revealing the exact details of this man's secret; something his daughter had told him alone on her death-bed. Mr. Woodcock however persisted. He announced, "This is the Devil's representative!" to which the voice lost all its sweetness and exploded in temper, reverting once more to the mannerisms of the previous days' threats of violence, and cursing them all. At this, Mr. Woodcock made his departure, presumably feeling vindicated. All the visitors there that night signed a sheet of paper, testifying to what they had heard, and everything that had happened that night. But more was to come; the voice was not finished yet. It demanded that a Clergyman be brought to the house. A Baptist clergyman called Reverend Bell was duly summoned; but the Reverend refused to engage in conversation with what he said was "The Devil," whereupon the furious voice called the Reverend, "A coward and all words..." Reverend Bell, the Ottawa Free Press reported, responded by trying to drive the devil out – but the devil did not take him seriously and told him to stick to his day job! Defeated, the Reverend left. After this, the voice told the crowd; "You don't believe I am an Angel because my voice is coarse. I tell the truth. I am not that person who used the dirty language. I am sent from God," and he began to sing in the most angelic tone. "Come to the saviour," he sung, "He is calling you to

Jesus, come, come to him brothers and sisters." All of those present later testified that it was the most divine voice they had ever heard. Some were even moved to tears by it. They were transfixed and deeply affected. However, at exactly 3 a.m., the voice told them it was now departing - but it would return one last time to see the children tomorrow, it said.

Sometime the next morning, the three Dagg children ran in from the fields, 'wild-eyed and fearfully excited.' Mary, the five-year-old daughter told their mother; "The beautiful man took Johnny in his arms, he went to Heaven and was all red." Their mother, very alarmed, asked her to describe what she saw. The children said that it was a man "dressed in white with ribbons and pretty things" all over his clothing, and "stars and gold on his head." His face was "lovely," they all agreed, and he had long white hair. They said he had bent down and scooped them all up into his arms. They said he told them that despite what Mr. Woodcock had said about him, he was an Angel, and he would "Show him!" The children said that he then rose up from the ground into the air and ascended "to Heaven" in a blaze of fire! He left, said the Ottawa Citizen, 'In a burst of streaking flame. Witnessed only by the children. A flight of fancy perhaps? Possibly. But harder to explain is the witness statements signed by 16 farmers and community leaders – from Clergymen to local politicians.' No matter how many times the children were asked, and no matter who asked them, the children never changed any details of their story or deviated from their account.

The strange man never returned after that, and life returned to as close to normality as was possible. One would imagine that many of those who had not been among the crowds of onlookers at the farm, would be very sceptical of the story that was told, and many may have laughed heartily about it, and yet it appears that Mr. Dagg's reputation remained intact after the events, for he went on to become the local Mayor. One story goes that Dina was sent away to live with her natural father, as there was always a lingering suspicion that because the strange man had been most drawn to her, she had somehow caused his attraction to her. Local historian Graham said there are no marriage or death records for Dina on file anywhere. However, according to the January 14th 1891 edition of The Times of Philadelphia, there is a strange addendum, and it would seem that Dina went to live with her uncle for a while, not her natural father. They say, 'To Thomas Dagg, related to George Dagg, the ghost is no joke but an unsolved mystery. At his home in Portage du Fort, the serious and religious man told of the ghost.' Looking back on the strange series of events 6 years earlier, Thomas 'claimed that a Showman came to the father and asked for Dina, the adopted girl. The father wouldn't let him have her and then the ghost began its work. Thomas told of Dina going to her uncle Willie Dagg at Portage du Fort and a man coming to the door with a note signed by George Dagg asking that Dina come home. The man left with Dina and she was never heard from again, said Mr. Dagg.'

Had the stranger tricked her by pretending her father was asking for her to come home? Who was this "Showman" who came to the door and led Dina away, never to be seen again? And what did he do with Dina?

Chapter Fifteen:

The Missing Genius

On May the 29th 1999, the remains of Philip Taylor Kramer were found. The one-time bass guitarist for the 1970's rock group 'Iron Butterfly' had been missing for four years. His disappearance and death is a mystery to this day.

Kramer's 1993 Ford Aerostar van was found at the bottom of a Malibu ravine by hikers in a canyon, about 1.5 miles east of the Pacific Coast Highway. His remains were found inside his van and they were later identified through dental records. His death would ultimately be ruled "Probable Suicide." However, his family hold strong doubts about this. His widow told the La Times back then, "He would never under any circumstances, for any reason allow himself to completely abandon the family he loves more than life itself."

Kramer had been bass player in the psychedelic group 'Iron Butterfly,' who'd been quite big back in the mid

'70's. By 1977 however, Kramer had decided to re-focus on furthering his education, and he completed a degree in Aerospace Engineering. He was a highly intelligent man who'd got straight A's all through High School. After gaining his degree he went to work for Northrup, a defence company, and Kramer worked on the MX missile guidance system as a Department of Defense contractor.

A couple of years later, he made a move into the computer industry, where he worked on early facial recognition development and communications development programs. To say he was intelligent was probably an understatement. He was quite possibly a computer genius.

Fast-forward to the day he disappeared, and on February the 12th 1995, Kramer drove to LA Airport where he had arranged to pick up a business associate, Mr Greg Martini and his wife in arrivals. However, after being at the airport for approximately 45 minutes, Kramer got back into his car and departed from the airport without waiting for his business associate to arrive.

After driving away from the airport, Kramer stopped and began to make a series of telephone calls. He called a former band member and close friend, Ron Busby, and said to him, "I'll see you on the other side." Then he called the police and said, "This is Philip Taylor Kramer. I'm going to kill myself. And I want everyone to know O.J Simpson is innocent. They did it." Then he disappeared.

48 months later, his skeletal remains were found at the bottom of the ravine in Decker Canyon; a place Maxim Magazine described as such; "If you ever need to dump a

corpse, you could do worse than Dekker Canyon. Located a 40-minute drive from LA, the rugged chasm is all but uninhabited. Best of all there's a thick screen of trees at the bottom. All you have to do is prop up the body in the front seat, release the parking brake and let em rip...'

Kramer's skeleton was discovered by 30-year-old Walter Lockewood, a fitness instructor and amateur photographer with a penchant for taking pictures of old abandoned cars. He'd heard stories over the years of cars being driven off the cliff there, and he'd ventured to the canyon to see if he could find any, thinking they would make cool photographs.

He'd taken a friend with him and that afternoon they had gone into the canyon in excitement. Despite the thick mass of over-grown trees and bushes, it had not taken them long to spot a pick-up truck, then a sedan. To their surprise, it began to creep them out a little bit. The cars were violently smashed from head-first dives off the road above. Then they spotted another vehicle partly hidden in the undergrowth. There were no licence plates on this one. It was an Aerostar van which was caved in on the driver's side. It too looked like it had come down off the cliff head-first. As they edged closer, they didn't like this adventure now. They thought they could see a leg bone. They didn't want to be there anymore and they hastily began to get out of there, with a plan to inform the police. As they walked through a gully, Lockewood trod on a skull. "I just let out the most primal shriek!" It was Kramer's skull.

How did Kramer end up dead at the bottom of the Canyon? When Kramer vanished in 1995, the Washington

Post wrote, 'Taylor Kramer, rock musician, rocket scientist, has vanished into thin air. He could be a suicide. A homicide. A runaway. An alien abductee.' Why would they mention "aliens"? Well, we shall discover that there was a lot more to Kramer than seen at first glance.

'He knew how to configure the flight path of a nuclear missile. He developed revolutionary technology. Student of theoretical physics, he pursued particles and equations,' and his disappearance, they say, 'became part of pop mythology dwelling in the same landscape as a living Elvis, the UFO crash at Rosewell, and the evil designs of the One World Government.'

Maxim's says, 'In his last days, Kramer was obsessively working on perfecting a top-secret 30-year-old formula, a Universal Equation he and his father believed could change the course of history: fast-than-light travel with a strange kind of gravitational vibration wilder than anything seen in Star Trek.' After Kramer vanished, The Washington Post said, 'He believed someday would permit objects to move faster than the speed of light at 'warp-speed' – making travel to the Stars possible. Is Kramer trapped by his own technological wizardry somewhere in cyberspace?'

Before Kramer vanished, he made approximately 16 telephone calls. In the call to friend Bushy he said, "I love you more than life itself," then hung up. Kramer had met Bushy when he'd gigged as a bouncer on the door of LA's Whisky-A-Go-Go, a thriving rock club which helped launch the careers of bands like The Doors. When Kramer joined Bushy's band, they had success, becoming the first band in history to have a Platinum album. Their hit song 'In a gadda da vida,' was unusually 17 minutes long, and was supposed to be called 'In the garden of Eden' but, according to Maxim magazine, the band's singer Doug Ingle had reportedly drunk a gallon of red wine during their recording session and could only slur the words of his idea for the title! It's a trippy, psychedelic tune. Music magazine said the group partied hard in those days, although Kramer himself, 6 foot 5 inches and handsome, worked out every day, and apparently did 1,000 sit-ups each morning. While his band-mates liked to party, Kramer preferred spending his time on tours scribbling complex mathematical formulas and talking about them. Said Bushy, "We'd stay up all night, write music and talk about his theories. He was talking stuff that was science fiction – about how you could not only communicate but also transport matter from A to B anywhere in the galaxy! Real beam me up stuff!"

According to Bushy, although the other band members had been into drugs and women, Kramer had eschewed this traditional Rockstar style in favour of long-nights spent on mathematical puzzles.

Kramer's father was just like him. They were both obsessed with proving that Einstein was wrong. Kramer's fascination for theoretical mathematics and physics began as a child when his father was professor of Engineering at Ohio State University. In the early 60's, his father Ray began a driven theoretical quest to conquer the boundaries of time and space. Kramer's father claimed, "Using the formula I discovered, you could reach the outer limits of the universe in less than a second."

'His greatest achievement he says, is his Universal Equation which promises to solve physics most intractable mysteries – a meta-theory that ties together black holes, quarks, and quantum mechanics into an all-encompassing package. He says, with it, information can be transmitted 16 times the speed of light – a potentially earth-shattering achievement that conventional science says is impossible.'

After Kramer gained his engineering degree, he got a job with 'top secret' clearance at Northrop as a department. In those days, his cubicle had to be taped shut when he was inside of it – so that his co-workers would know they could not cross the boundary. This was to ensure his top-secret work was protected. The precise details of exactly what Kramer did is, of course still classified, so we do not know exactly what he was doing. He did not stay very long at Northrop however, and he became an entrepreneur, branching out on his own. He set up a company called 'Total Multimedia,' a high-tech company that pioneered work in developing video compression technology that would turn music into digital form, by developing a fractal data compression technology for CD-ROMs. Kramer had also married and now had a daughter and step-son. Sadly however, despite being full of ground-breaking ideas, his company struggled financially, even with backers who included Randy Jackson, one of Michael Jackson's brothers. In 1994, the company went bankrupt, and as a result of this the company was restructured, with a new

CEO brought in. This is said to have been the time when things began to get strange.

The new CEO was a man called Peter Olsen, and with him came an adviser – a Paraguayan shaman who would give Olsen psychic and "channelled advice." It was around this time, according to Kramer's colleagues and family, that Kramer began to believe he could communicate telepathically with Extra Terrestrials. When Olsen joined the company, he informed all employees that they must read the book 'The Celestine Prophecy,' a New-Age book that explains human consciousness as merely one form of flowing energy and vibration that merges with other energy fields in the material and spiritual world. The LA Times called it 'a book that asserts that enlightened people vibrate at such a high frequency they disappear.' In one of the end chapters, the book explains that this is apparently possible! As for Olsen, 'Word circulated among some employees that he proudly declared himself to be half-human half-alien.' Kramer's sister Kathy said her brother began to claim he spoke with aliens frequently. "He talked of supernovas, earthquakes, all events having no coincidences. He was calling the math 'scared.' I worried that he was having visions. I fear he had some kind of breakdown." When 1995 came, Kramer was doing 16-hour days – not just for his company, but he had become determined to prove the theory he and his father had come up with. His father had suggested Kramer could combine data compression with gravity waves for communication systems, by using their theory. On February the 10th, two days before he vanished,' the LA Times says, co-worker Dan Shields 'sat Kramer down and begged him to listen to what Shields feared was Taylor's impending mental breakdown.'

'Instead, Kramer told Shields about his work and said he was fine, although he agreed he would get some rest. Shields said, "He tried to bridge these three things - New Age Spirituality, his father's physics formula, and computer technology. We had a pact. He would call me Saturday and Sunday and we'd talk." And Kramer did do this. "He was much more grounded. No statements of spirituality or universe or extra-terrestrials. Very lucid, clear, calm." However, it was not to last. He'd spent weeks barely sleeping and suddenly Kramer had a "Eureka" moment. Kramer announced to his friends and family that he'd finally had a break-through and that something "amazing" was about to happen. On February the 11th, Kramer phoned good friend Lori Pietsch and told her, "I have to be very, very careful. I was able to decipher the code - it was heavily encrypted. People are going to want what I'm working on. We have to get off the planet."

On February the 12th, the day of his disappearance, Kramer worked out for two hours in the morning, then drove to LA airport where he was due to meet his business associate. Instead, he left the airport without picking him up, phoned his wife and told her he had a big surprise, then dialled 911 and told them he was going to kill himself. He called his wife again and said, "Whatever happens, I'll always be with you." In all, he made 16 phone calls. Had Kramer finally had a nervous breakdown? Had his obsession finally driven him to the brink of insanity? Or, had his New-Age reading fired his imagination into overdrive and he had lost any sense of reality? Or had he discovered something so shocking, so valuable, that people would literally kill for what he knew? He told his wife he was not going to see her "On this side." In other words, it would seem he meant he would see her in Heaven. After calling his wife, he stopped off at Los Robles hospital to see his terminally-ill father-in-law. He pulled a small device from his pocket, and he said, "It's all right here. I know you don't understand – but it's all right." The device turned out to be a child's viewing lense that replicates and fragments anything you view as you look through it. Later, Kramer called 911 from his car. The operator asked, "Can I help you?" Kramer replied, "Yes you can. This is Philip Kramer. I am going to kill myself." His father later said that this was a code for "Help." But how would 911 have known he needed help and was sending a coded message? – They didn't know he had a code! And how would his father know Kramer was using his code and needed help, if Kramer called 911 and not his father? Isn't that an odd way of doing it, if the person you are telling doesn't know you are talking in code! His father said Kramer had told him that this code meant Kramer was under the control of others. But how would his father get this message? Why didn't he phone his father and give him the code? His father said that Kramer had told him, "If I ever say I'm going to kill myself; don't believe it. I'm gonna be needing help."

Why did Kramer say, "O.J. Simpson is innocent – They did it?" The LA Times in their investigations in the 1980's said Kramer had been hired to review surveillance footage in his trial, 'to analyse the authenticity of a video tape that the FBI and the DEA had on the O.J. Simpson murder trial.' Why did he say, "They did it?" Who were they?

Researcher for Skeptic Magazine, Frederick Rice said, 'The quote about killing himself is not accurate. He informed his family that he was going to endeavour to appear to have killed himself so that "them" that he believed was going to come after he and his father to "silence" his discovery would refrain from doing so, but also, according to the transcripts, refrain from harming his family. Previous calls to his family stated that he was going to try to "lead them away" from his family, fake his own death for his own safety and that of his family.' His friend Lori said that when Kramer told her they had to get off the planet, "I'm convinced he was under mind control or psychic attack." Was Kramer under physical control when he made that 911 call? Was Kramer being forced by someone to tell the police he was going to commit suicide? Former LA Police Officer & DEA Agent Chuck Carter, who was hired as a Private Eye by the Kramer family said, "Whatever happened in his head at the airport or whatever happened at the airport, I've got a feeling we'll learn from Kramer himself." Of course, that became impossible when Kramer turned up dead four years later.

In the days before Kramer disappeared, he'd warned his wife he might be in danger. His friends at work said Kramer believed his recent breakthrough of solving the theoretical psychics equation was worth "Billions." He told his wife they'd have to move into a house with high walls. "He was scared that people were trying to get at him," she said. He became prone to outbursts like, "God is a scientist. A perfect scientist! Chaos is perfect order!" The day before he vanished, he told his sister "You've got to be centred. If you're centred, you'll be saved when the supernova happens, and they come." He said he had channelled the Tenth insight from The Celestine Prophecy and had called his friend Lori and asked her to transcribe it as he channelled it.

After Kramer's disappearance, his company, Total Multimedia hired a PI to search for him, while COE Olsen used his Paraguayan Shaman to try to channel Kramer's whereabouts. His sister went on any daytime talk shows that would have her, to talk about her brother's disappearance, in the hope of viewers calling in with tips or clues. An Austrian psychic wrote to Kramer's sister telling her that Kramer was 'Alive and well and being worshipped as a god on an Indian Reservation near San Diego!' The Washington Post said his family 'Checked that out. They visited several purported UFO landing sites, and also tried Sedona, the New Age capital. No signs of Kramer. Some credible sightings emerged in the early days. A pawnshop manager in California swore that Kramer came in and talked about computers. A woman holding a yard sale said a very tall man approached her, trying to buy clothes, but she didn't have any sizes big enough.' Others thought they saw him in a bar. A woman at a school bus stop on Mulholland Drive said a man looking like Kramer, wearing filthy clothes and with matted hair approached her and asked her, "Are you waiting for someone?" An LA Times report in 1996 said, 'At a Ralphs supermarket in Agoura Hills, an elderly couple was approached by a very tall man fitting his description. "I'm in trouble and need to call my family and only have 40 cents. Can you help me?" The man figured him to be a bum and said, "No," but his wife told us she later scolded her husband because he didn't seem like a beggar. She told us he seemed genuine, that he was polite.' Kramer's wife received a phone call, 'From a man whose voice she is convinced is Kramer's, but it is deeply stressed, as she puts it, the voice of a person who is "out of it". Faintly, the caller said, "Hello ….. Hello …. Hello ….."'

Seargent David Paige for the Ventura County Sheriff's Department said, "There's no crime here. All we have is a despondent individual who said he'd commit suicide," while his wife told the Newspaper, "He's out there but his mind is gone." Sheriff's helicopters searched the Santa Monica Mountains and the San Fernando Valley – but they found nothing.

Two years passed and the LA Times interviewed his family again. 'Family members say they will dismiss no scenario, no matter how outlandish. UFOs? It's possible. Or maybe he is in a government protection program? Or has been hijacked or kidnapped or suffered amnesia and can't find his way home. Although dismissive of theories he was kidnapped because of bad business dealings, some in his family say it's possible he may have been kidnapped for what he knew. 'Chuck Carter, the Private Investigator discovered that Kramer owed money and was in debt. "He owed hundreds of thousands," and had "exhausted all avenues to borrow more." His sister Kathy said Kramer and CEO Olsen were interested in this faster-than-light travel so they could escape the supernova Kramer said would destroy planet earth. Business partner Tom Simpson told the LA Times, "He came up with the idea that for some reason he knew there was a supernova that was going to destroy the planet in 4 years. So, the technology that he was working on was imperative to us to get off the planet to save the human race. And he seemed to believe it." His sister told the Times, "He said if you were 'centered,' and he would make this hand motion down the centre of your face and body, if you're centered, we'll be taken care of, everyone will be fine, everyone that's centered."

Congressman James Traficant appealed to the FBI to investigate. "Someone may have grabbed him," he believed. "There's some funny things," he said. "A foreign power might have "abducted, apprehended, compromised, or somehow brainwashed Kramer," or, "possible domestic agencies could use Kramer's extraordinary knowledge for nefarious purposes." The congressman urged the FBI to analyse the 911 call Kramer made to determine if Kramer had made the call voluntarily, or perhaps under duress. Traficant felt that because Kramer had formerly worked on nuclear missile paths, he could have been a target; although Kramer had left that work several years before he disappeared. The congressman believed Kramer could have been snatched by terrorists to be brainwashed "to carry out a nuclear strike." Or, that his own Government wanted Kramer's secret knowledge. "The evidence indicates Kramer could have been abducted at the airport and forced to make a series of calls to make it seem that he committed suicide," said the Congressman. Meanwhile, the police were stumped. "Pick a scenario, any scenario," said Detective Tom Bennett of the Sheriff's department. Was Kramer followed to the airport that day? Did he think someone was after him in the airport? Did he encounter someone there that made him feel unsafe or threatened? Were his family threatened? Did he feel like the walls were closing in on him and he could see no way out? Did Kramer have priceless secrets? Best friend Bushy believed Kramer was 'disappeared.' "After his breakthrough, we wouldn't need cell phones, landlines, or satellites." Bushy implied big business could be behind his friend's vanishing. The Washington Post however said, of Kramer's theories, 'What makes this argument invalid is the fact that it is based upon a myth. Real scientists say it can't happen. Based on what they know, we'll never get to the stars. And the aliens can't get here. The distances are simply too great. Dr. Milton A. Rothman, former professor of Physics states that for such things to be possible, a new particle responsible for carrying a new force would have to be discovered; yet were such particle to actually exist, it would have been inferred by experimentation long before now,' and 'we must make do with the forces that exist!'

Kramer believed he could 'channel' communication to aliens on other planets. Kramer told friends that he spoke to other planets and to God. He sounds like Tesla. On January the 4th 1901, The San Francisco Examiner reported, 'World speaks to world with mysterious signals through vast space. Tesla, the electrician, says he received a message from mars. Nikola Tesla has had the first call of the century from a neighbouring planet. He has communicated with Mars, he declares, while on Pike's Peak delving into the mysteries of the wireless transmission of electrical energy. The summons was faint, but, according to Tesla, not to be mistaken. A new voice from a planet, millions of miles removed, was spoken over one of the myriad of unwired telephones of the universe, and there in the fathomless calm of night, the voice at last found a listener and world spoke to world in language strange at first, but sure to be clearer, says Tesla.'

When Kramer's remains were found at the bottom of the Canyon, his sister Kathy said she wasn't convinced it was even his body they had found. The police said they couldn't tell how fast the van had been going when it plummeted off the cliff. They couldn't tell if Kramer had been wearing a seat-belt. His autopsy showed many broken bones in his chest, which were consistent with a head-on car crash. The coroner said his cause of death was from 'blunt trauma and other unknown reasons.' Kramer apparently knew the canyon well, and it was one of the first places that was searched after his disappearance. At the time, no sign of him was found. Had Kramer been there all that time? Or had he been elsewhere during the 4 years he was missing? Had he been held somewhere? His family all believed it was impossible that Kramer would have killed himself. He had a young daughter, a wife, a father. None believed it was something he would ever do.

According to the Washington Post, Glen Mavis, who worked with Kramer back at Northrop said, "Whatever got him was something that he couldn't deal with – whether it was an outside force that came down on him or ….."

Detective Tom Bennett, who handled the case for Ventura Sheriff's Department said; "There's some funny things here... officially the case is still open...."

In 1996, The LA Times wrote, 'The day before he disappeared, Philip Kramer thought he would take his kids for a bite to eat. Finding only 40 cents in his pocket, he turned to his dad Ray and asked for a few dollars. Ray did what he never did: He told his son no. "It wasn't the money. It was Taylor. He was exhausted, burnt out, shot. I laughed and told him to go home and get some sleep."' He did, but only fitfully. His wife said he got up a few times that night, including one occasion where he was back at his computer running equations again. "It seemed like he was going without sleep entirely for days." In the last calls he made to his wife, his voice had a different tone says reporter Leonard Reed, 'Without the characteristic upbeat lilt; yet energized to the point of sounding out of breath. In one call, Kramer asked Jennifer to tell Martini – if Martini were to phone her – to take a cab from the airport to the Hyatt. Kramer said he would meet everyone there an hour later than planned, at 2 pm, with the "Biggest surprise."' At 11.59 am from somewhere in the San Fernando Valley on the Ventura Freeway,' Kramer made the 911 call. The family's PI Chuck Carter told Reed, "I've never seen a case like this. If you're 6 foot 5, getting from point A to B without being noticed is difficult to do. I'll tell you, I haven't a clue. The guy didn't have an enemy. The guy was an educated family man – I checked him out. It is very unusual in that there is absolutely no evidence."

Kramer's 'Eureka' moment happened two weeks before he vanished. His wife was so concerned about his sleeplessness during this time that she had asked him, what was he working on exactly? He told her, "Imagine being able to flash up a picture of a missing child on this computer screen, or even a part of a picture, and with this new equation being able to find that child in a fraction of a second. It's so simple that no-one has discovered it. It's been here the whole time." Did someone want this technology? Was Kramer threatened to hand over his technology to spare the lives of his family? Did he refuse and see no option but to kill himself, taking the secrets of his technology with him? Or, was Kramer simply so sleep-deprived, so over-worked and in such a state of paranoia that he accidentally drove off the edge of the road into the canyon?

Chapter Sixteen:

Who were he Children in the Polaroid?

In 1988, Tara Calico was a busy young woman. She worked part-time at a bank in town, was studying for a degree in psychology, and around these commitments she fitted regular work-outs or participated in sports. Most mornings she went for bike rides, and on this particular day, September the 20th 1988, she set out on her usual morning ride from her home in Belen, New Mexico. Before she left, she asked her mother to look out for her when it got to midday and if she wasn't back by then, she asked her mother to come and pick her up. Tara said this because she was concerned about being late for work. In the past she'd got a puncture on her bike and had been delayed.

When midday came and went and her daughter didn't return home, Tara's mother duly set out in her car to go find her daughter and bring her and the bicycle back home. However, as Tara's mother drove along the route her daughter always took, she couldn't see any sign of Tara. She drove back home, assuming that she had missed her daughter somewhere and that she would be back home by now. When she reached home however, there was no sign of Tara or her bike. Her mother immediately called the police.

A patrol car quickly arrived and the policemen started searching for Tara along the route she always took. They could not find here either but they did find a cassette tape lying in the road, that looked like it had probably come out of her Walkman stereo. Other than that, there were no other signs of Tara, apart from some bike tracks. The road Tara had been cycling on was a very straight road with very few cross-sections. There were no buildings and no trees. It was an open, barren landscape. There wasn't really anywhere for her to be if she wasn't on the road.

As the police extended their search area to a distance of nearly twenty miles away, they came across a Walkman portable stereo lying in the middle of the road. When they showed this to her Mother, she said it was Tara's. Her mother believed then that her daughter had been trying to leave clues and a trail to follow. This section of the road was close to a remote Campground called John F Kennedy. The trail ended there, at the base of the Manzano Mountain.

When police canvassed the area near Tara's home, witnesses said they had last seen Tara at around midday, in a spot less than two miles from her home. Someone said they had seen a pickup truck close behind her, but other than that, the trail went cold.

A year passed by with no further leads or clues about the girl's disappearance. The police had searched everywhere, questioned everyone, but no other information came. Then, in June 1989, hundreds of miles away in a parking lot outside a grocery store in Florida, a lady parked her car and walked into the store. When she returned, a white truck that had been parked next to her was now gone, but what she found in the empty parking space was something terrible. It was a Polaroid picture with a harrowing scene. Two children were lying on a bed, both bound and gagged. There was a boy who looked to be in early adolescence, and an older girl who looked to be in her teens. They were both staring into the camera with anxious, frightened expressions and the image was horrifying. She called the police immediately, telling them that the photograph must have been dropped by the man she had seen in the driver's seat of the white van as she parked. She described the man as having dark hair and a moustache. She said the van had no windows and a sliding door on one side. The police responded immediately, setting up road blocks to try to find his van, but it was too late. They did not find it and they believed he must have already left the area. Photographic analysis of the photo determined that it had been taken recently.

When Tara's mother was shown the photograph, she was immediately convinced that the girl in the photo was her missing daughter. The parents and family of a missing boy were also convinced that the boy in the picture with her was their missing son too. He had also gone missing in New Mexico, in the same year as Tara. Prior to Tara's disappearance, 9-year-old Michael Henley had been staying at a campsite in the Cibola National Park in the Zuni Mountains, less than fifty miles from where Tara lived. He had gone there with his Dad and a friend of his father to hunt turkeys.

They had only been at the campsite for a short while and were still setting up when his father realised that young Michael had disappeared. They quickly started looking for him, thinking he must have gone off wandering, but they couldn't see him anywhere nearby. Quickly they found a Ranger and reported him missing.

The official search for the missing boy started immediately, but a sudden storm came in and this made it extremely difficult to look for him in the wilderness. Snow was falling fast, despite it having been quite warm earlier in the day, and the child had only thin clothing on. Nearly five hundred people searched for the boy, with the National Guard joining the Park Rangers and the police and many volunteers, and they all spanned out over a ten-mile radius. Even air searches were carried out overhead.

Tracks thought to be Michael's were found in the snow but no-one could be absolutely sure they were his. Despite bloodhounds assisting the search, there were too many other scents because of the sheer number of people looking for him, and the dogs found it impossible to pick up on the boy's trail.

Despite a week-long search, the little boy was not found. Most of those involved in the search believed that he must have wandered off and become quickly lost and disoriented in an unfamiliar environment. Unable to find his way back to the camp ground, he had then succumbed to the cold and died of exposure and eventually his body would have suffered natural predation. They thought that when hypothermia began to set in, he may have tried to burrow to seek shelter and crawled into any enclosed area he could find among the trees. Yet still no remains were found.

And then came the Polaroid photograph, which both families said contained the bound and gagged images of their children. As the Lowell Sun Newspaper reported on July 31st 1989, 'Mystery photo launches probe. Parent's believe captive youths are their children. Relatives of two New Mexico youths who vanished last year said they're pretty sure their children were shown gagged in a mysterious photograph that appeared on national television last week. The parents of Tara Calico and Michael Hanley Jr believe the picture is the first evidence that the missing youths are still alive, perhaps in captivity in Florida.' The photos were analysed by the FBI and even Scotland Yard, and it was determined that this was Tara. Sheriff Ed Craig said, 'It's the best lead we've had in ten months."

For Tara's local Sheriff Rene Riviera however, over the years since Tara vanished, he never gave up investigating. He believed that from what he uncovered; her abductor was someone a lot closer to home. He became convinced it was some local boys, whose names he knew. They had run her off the road, he believed, buried her, probably killing her by accident and then panicking to cover it up. However, what he lacked was solid evidence. A petition on Change.org was started by staff writer of the

Albuquerque Journal, Leslie Linthicum. '"The individuals who did the harm to Tara, knew who she was," Rivera told me. "They knew who she was, and they're all local individuals. And I believe that the parents (of the attackers) were some of the people that helped the individuals with hiding the truth or hiding the body or trying to escape prosecution." Riviera said, "She was a real pretty girl. A lot of guys wanted to talk to her, and while she was riding the bike, they went up to try to talk to her, try to grab her, whatever, while she was on the bike." Rivera said he had "enough information to get arrest warrants for the two boys — now men," but that "It's kind of hard to make a case without a body."'

As for the missing boy in the polaroid, Michael Henley's father said at the time that even his son's best friend said it was definitely the boy. Although the Father said he himself wasn't completely sure, he also didn't know if that was because he didn't want to accept that this was his child, pictured in such a vulnerable and bleak condition. Then a new twist came in 1990. The boy's remains were discovered approximately eight miles from the campground in the mountains. A person on a horse had come across human bones in a thick copse of trees. Dental records determined that this was Michael's remains. No cause of death could be given to explain how he had ended up dead eight miles away, although exposure to the elements seemed the most likely scenario.

It now seemed unlikely that the boy had been taken to Florida and photographed and then returned to the area in which he disappeared from in the mountain. If someone had abducted him, the man in the white van for example, why would he go to the effort of returning Michael's body to the area in which he had gone missing? - Unless he wanted the death to look like he had died from exposure. But why take the risk of being seen? Police said that as far as they were concerned, they were ruling out foul play, and that the boy in the polaroid was definitely not Michael. If it wasn't Michael, then who was the boy in the photograph?

Adding further to the mystery is that two more Polaroid photographs of a woman that looked like Tara emerged. The first photo was found near a construction site in Montecito, California. It is a blurry close-up photo of a girl's face with tape covering her mouth and her head lying on a striped light blue fabric that looks like a pillow. The pattern of the pillow looks very similar to the pattern in the 1st photo of Tara and the young boy. The 2nd second photograph shows a young woman who is loosely bound in gauze. Her eyes are covered with more gauze and she is wearing large black-framed glasses. She is on an Amtrak train and a male passenger is seated beside her. The man looks much older than her and he is holding onto her. Her hands are tied together. Her legs are bound but the material is hanging loose off her legs, as though it has been undone, or, hastily tied. Her face is almost obscured and held horizontally facing the roof of the train so it is hard to see her face clearly. Investigators determined that the roll of film used to take this photo was not available until after February 1990. Tara's mother believed this second photograph could be Tara; or, it could be someone's idea of a sick joke. Perhaps it could even have been a young woman who looked like Tara, larking around with a male companion on a long train journey. Tara's mother agreed, but she felt different about the close-up photo of Tara's face on a pillow in the other photograph. Tara's step-sister thought that it looked very much like her in both of the new photos. "They had a striking, uncalming resemblance. Keep in mind our family has had to identify many other photographs and all but those three were ruled out. If I had to say yes or no definitively: Yes, that is her. Does it make sense? No. I still look at it and it looks exactly like her — But it really does not make sense."

Then came yet another twist in 2009. Two more photographs materialised. This time, they were sent to the police and the local newspapers in New Mexico. The first photograph shows a young boy who has black pen drawn over his mouth, making it appear as though his mouth has been gagged, just like in the original Polaroid photo from twenty years ago. The second photograph is the same as the original polaroid discovered on the ground in the parking mall in Florida in 1989. They were sent to the police and media around the time of the anniversary of Tara's disappearance. Who was the boy in the photograph, with the black ink over his mouth?

Were these photos sent from their abductor, taunting the authorities, showing them that he'd got away with it, and now had another victim too? There was nothing that would help the authorities. The letters containing the photos had been posted in Albuquerque; but that was all they knew. The authorities said they were not sure if the boy in the new photograph was the same as the boy in the original photograph with Tara. If it wasn't, then who was this new boy? Had he been abducted too? Who was the boy in the original photo from 1989? And what happened to them all?

Chapter Seventeen:

What happened to Henry McCabe?

When Henry McCabe disappeared, he left what can only be described as the most bone-chilling voicemail. He is screaming, pleading, and growling in raw, animalistic agony. Along with these sounds is a noise in the background that sounds indefinably mechanical. As we listen to it, we do not know what is happening to him. Even more chilling is the moment another voice can be heard, telling Henry in a cold, emotionless, detached voice, "Stop it." Fifty-five days later, Henry's body was found in an isolated creek. His body had no wounds, no trauma, no injuries. How could this be possible after Henry's harrowing, visceral voicemail? What was it that took Henry to the gaping, echoing abyss of unremitting terror? And who, or what took him on that terrible one-way journey? "This is what they did to my son. Henry paid for you to learn the lesson," said his mother; but what does she mean?

Henry was a 32-year-old émigré from Liberia and a father of two. He worked for the City of Minnesota as a tax auditor. At 2.05 am on Labor Day, September the 7th 2015, Henry McCabe was dropped off from a nightclub in Minnesota by an acquaintance. The acquaintance said Henry asked him for a ride home when they were at the Povlitzki Nightclub, commonly known as 'POV's' and located on Highway 65 in Spring Lake Park, and which apparently goes by the name of Club 'C'est La Vie' on Sunday nights, which it was that night.

This acquaintance, William 'Papus' Kennedy says he offered to take Henry home but that at some point in the journey, Henry suggested that he be dropped off at a Gas Station instead, and said that he would walk from there. "Brother, just drop me to the gas station. I'm going to be fine; this whole area is my area," Papus said Henry told him. When Henry was dropped off that night, he had no money on him and no keys to get in his house. His friends told the police they had taken Henry's car keys and wallet off him because they believed he was drunk and should not drive home or buy any more drinks. Instead of calling him a cab or escorting him home, his friends let Henry go with Papus. Did his friends realize he had left the nightclub without his house keys? He would not be able to get in when he got home, but as it transpired, Henry never made it home.

According to Mounds View Police Department Chief Tom Kinney, at 2.28 a.m. a call was made from Henry's cell phone to his wife Kareen McCabe, who at the time was staying with relatives in California. According to a search warrant affidavit later filed in Ramsey Court District, in this phone call to his wife, Henry "is yelling, screaming and making weird grunting noises." Kare News reported, 'Those who know Henry shared the recording in the hope that whoever knows what happened will come forward.' It is hard to listen to, and it is hard to decipher. 'There are 2 minutes of bizarre noises, including growls, screams and moans. There's very few actual words.'

Kareen told ABC News, "I try to picture where he was, what it might have been like, what circumstances would have made him sound like that." The police sent the audio of Henry to a local FBI office "for further cleaning up and analysis." His wife said, "One word he said was "Police." He said certain words, like "They are afraid."' The audio of Henry is still on the internet available to listen to and it is horrific. When Henry called his wife, Kareen tried to talk to him, but he did not respond. It would later transpire that Henry had accidentally called her. Or had he? The Minnesota Recorder reported, 'Kareen notified Henry's family members that in the early hours of September the 7th, Henry's phone pocket-dialed her and Henry was heard screaming in distress and stated that someone "shot him."' Had Henry 'pocket-dialled' her without realizing she could hear his every cry, every scream? Or, did someone else have hold of his phone? Did someone else want Henry's wife to hear him screaming, growling, desperate; to taunt her, to grind her senses in an onslaught of audial torment? There is confusion in these reports, conflicting information, muddied attempts to make sense of what they heard. What has not been disputed is the intensity of the primal voicemail he left that night. There are indefinable noises. His screams are worse than any horror movie scream. They said it sounds almost non-human.

When Henry's call came through that night in the early hours, his wife Kareen used her landline phone to call Henry's elder brother, Timothy Borbor, on his cell phone. Due to the time of night however, Henry's brother didn't pick up, and he didn't check his phone until the next day. Then he saw the missed call notification and listened to the voicemail that had been left for him, and he too could hear Henry's screams and growls coming from Kareen's cell phone. As he listened to his brother, Borbor understood that something was very wrong. After failing to get hold of Henry himself, he quickly contacted the police and filed a missing person's report. The Police then listened to Henry's voicemail, but Henry didn't give any clues about where he was when he was screaming. The police had to wait for Henry's cell phone provider to give them the records showing which cell tower Henry was closest to when his phone had last 'pinged.'

When news of Henry's voicemail hit the media, Fox 9 reported, 'Most of the message is unintelligible – it is in stark contrast to the hard-working family man that many knew him to be.' Many wondered, had Henry's acquaintance played a role in his disappearance? William 'Papus' Kennedy, in the face of growing suspicion and innuendo said, "I am willing even if it costs me to pay for it, to take a lie detector test." He was protesting his innocence. He told Kare 11 News, "I have no motive. I don't want to hurt Henry or anyone. I really wish Henry would come out somewhere alive and explain the true story himself." But Henry was no-where to be seen. "I want to clear my name," said Kennedy. "We were not friends, more like acquaintances. I wish I had never given him a ride... I wish I never did." In fact, when Henry was later found, the Police would say, "This is not a criminal case and we don't have any suspects."

According to the Ramsey Court District records, Papus Kennedy 'told police the other friends took McCabe's wallet in an effort to stop him buying more drinks because he was "very intoxicated."' This was most unexpected, because according to his friends and family, Henry was never known to drink excessively, nor did he take drugs. If his friends are to be believed when they say he was intoxicated, why would Henry have drunk so uncharacteristically that night? One possible reason could have been because he was troubled. According to newspaper reports at the time, Henry had apparently sent a bad cheque for his last rent payment, and it was also reported that Henry had received a poor performance review at his work. Could Henry have been suffering emotional anguish and concern about being able to support and provide for his family and keep a roof over their heads? Drinking alcohol can lower our inhibitions and open the floodgates of our emotions – good or bad. Was Henry in a bad way that night? Did it all become too much for him? People who are worried disappear all the time. A pressure-cooker builds inside of them and the stress of trying to just get by can feel unrelenting and sometimes a person feels no option but to simply leave, to get away from a situation they cannot see a solution to, and they walk off to another life, or sometimes to death. And yet, if

Henry had been feeling that all hope in his life was gone, why would he walk six miles to a spot only accessible through thick inhospitable vegetation, in pitch darkness, toward a creek that was so isolated few even knew it was there, and end his life there? For that is where he was found.

The crime scene photos show this location. There is no footpath to lead him to where he was found. It is a bleak landscape of tall dense trees and thick brambles. Had Henry tried to cut-through this area, to get home? And yet it was no-where near where he had been dropped off, and no-where near home, and it led only to the cold depths of the water. It was not an easy route to get through, and it was not a route to anywhere other than desolation.

During the police searches for Henry in the 54 days he was missing, Papus said he had dropped Henry off at the Super America Service Station. It was not until much later that Papus changed this to the Holiday Service Station. The Mounds View police department said the last call made from Henry's cell phone pinged off a tower near Silver Lake Road and Mississippi Street in New Brighton. 'That's about 5 minutes from the Super America gas station where William Papus Kennedy said he dropped off Henry on that morning,' reported the local news. Surveillance footage later found showed Henry at the Holiday Convenience store and Gas station, his family announced. Some said it was very suspicious that Papus had given the wrong gas station to the police, but Papus said he had simply been mistaken and that he did not know the area well-enough to remember. Perhaps Papus had been confused, or perhaps Papus had been drinking too that night. Perhaps they had consumed drugs that night, and he didn't want to get into trouble? Whichever the case, Papus' mistake had sent searchers in the wrong direction, although in fact, despite the weeks of searching, it was a kayaker who came across Henry's body in the end, not any of the search parties.

After Henry disappeared, authorities and volunteers spent weeks organising searches to try to find him. Reporter Issa Mansaray said; 'The search for Henry continued unabated on Saturday October 3rd, almost 4 weeks after he went missing. Many volunteers including family spent hours knocking on doors and distributing flyers, in hopes of finding McCabe, yet he remains nowhere to be found.' County Sheriff dive teams searched bodies of water around Henry's last known tracks, while MCPS directed Search and Rescue efforts for three months. One of the volunteers who joined the search, Magdalene Meyongar said, "A grown man just disappeared for weeks and is no place to be found. He just vanished. This is very scary."

Then, his body was found in Rush Lake by a passing kayaker. His body was half-in, half-out of the Lake. It was November the 2nd 2015, 55 days after he'd vanished. Dave Singleton of MCPS said, "I was dispatched to Rush Lake to observe the recovery of a body that had been there for some time." The distance between where Henry was dropped off and the Creek, was 6 miles. Ramsey county Medical Examiner's office said the 33-year old's death "Does not appear to be suspicious," and Police Chief Kinney said, "But the cause remains undetermined."

Minnesota Pioneer Press reported, 'McCabe's older brother Timothy Borbor said he's unsure what to think. New Brighton police conducted a ground search near where the body was found and also searched Rush Lake via boat but found nothing that could be considered evidence.' "Henry was not an isolated person in the middle of the dark," said Pastor Marie Vah, "And yet that is where he found himself.... if he was alone." People were perplexed. At Henry's Memorial, 'Mourners were led to the site on Rush Lake where his body was reportedly dumped. Many placed flowers there and discussed the distance from where he was last seen to where he was found in the lake, 55 days after his disappearance.'

At the Vigil, many asked how Henry would have walked there. "It doesn't appear that he will come here on his own. We believe he was not brought here on his own free will. It appears someone brought him to this location," said Singleton. "It is not a location that you can get to easily, just off the main street." Honourable Jackson George, Liberia's acting consul general in Minnesota said, "We have a tradition; no grown person will walk into that place to kill himself." Suicide was not a tradition, was not something a Liberian would do, he meant. From the Embassy's point of view, he said, "We're not going to close this case until justice is done." Kareen, his wife asked, "Why did he have to die like this? He just cares about people – caring for those that are oppressed and in need." Material things were nothing to Henry, she said. "I want justice for my husband. He didn't deserve to die. There is a God and he knows what happened and hates an injustice … whoever did this, God will deal with you."

There were those in the Liberian community who wondered; could this be something to do with their home country? Henry and many others had emigrated to America to escape the Civil War violence in their home. Yet his autopsy found no signs of trauma on his body and no signs of foul play. It was determined that Henry had died from fresh water drowning. CBS local for Minnesota reported, 'The Ramsey County Medical Examiner released the final autopsy report, ruling it a drowning,' but 'the case remains an open and active investigation.'

The Spokesman Recorder reported, 'As the family and community prepare to lay Henry to rest, questions still linger as to how he really died and why no trace of a crime can be found.'

Seyon Nyanwieh, lead organiser of the community search and friend of the family, said that Henry couldn't have gone to where his body was found "all by himself," to a location that he pointed out is very isolated and dark after 6 pm. "Someone dropped him in the water," was his conclusion. Pastor Success Roberts, who led prayers at the site where they found Henry's body said, "This is where they found our friend. You can't expect a father, a man with no bad record, to just come and find himself there in Rush Lake." Long-time friend David Kessel said, "I don't think I can sleep tonight." People were confused, scared.

The FBI had tried to clean-up Henry's phone call, but it was no use. All they could still hear was screaming and growling and weird mechanical noises. The Recorder said, 'Police chiefs said the manner of death could have been homicide or suicide, that they don't currently have an answer.' New Brighton police chief Bob Jacobson said, "We may not be able to tell you everything." They weren't hiding anything, they said; they simply didn't know what happened. Mount View police chief Kinney said, "This case is unique and remains an investigation as to what might have happened to Henry."

The only evidence available was Henry's recorded phone call. It lasted for approximately 2 minutes. At one point, his wife said she thinks it sounded like he said he got shot; yet there were no gun-shot wounds on his body. There were no wounds at all. Why did he think he had been shot? What else could feel like a gun-shot delivered at close range, or from a distance? His wife believes it sounded like he was walking when he phoned her. What were the eerie mechanical grinding noise in the background? It did not sound like a truck. It sounded deeper, fiercer, terrifying. It was unrecognisable, and many have tried to work out what that noise was. Some said it sounded positively unnatural, and not of this world; that it sounded like it came from hell itself. Did Henry walk to the creek alone? Or was he taken to the creek? Whose was the voice that said, so calmly and coldly; "Stop it"? Could it have been Henry's own voice? His wife and family did not think so. It didn't sound like Henry, and Henry couldn't talk; he could only scream. Was someone there with him? Or, two people? Was there one man telling Henry to stop it, or was another man telling his accomplice to stop it? Henry had no injuries, now wounds, no trauma. What was being done to him that would cause such torturous pain, and yet leave no marks? Was a Taser being used on him perhaps? Or was he simply being forced under the water?

Why were there no marks on his head or neck, if someone was drowning him? His survival instincts would have made him fight, resist. And we hear no splashes, no coughing, no gasps for breath. Could the mechanical noise simply have been Henry's own lips vibrating together? In fear, or from the cold? Yet it was so loud, so vibratory, so grinding.

What could cause such pain yet leave no marks? Is there any possibility that Henry was being tasered? A taser can incapacitate a person and it can really hurt. Do they leave any marks? ABC News Health from May the 29th 2018 reported on the effect on the human body when it is tasered. 'On skin, the most common affects are superficial burns or small puncture wounds, caused by the metal probes that deliver the current not being immediately pulled off after a person has been tased. Scrapes are often seen across the skin surface because the person shocked by the Taser may convulse uncontrollably.' A study in the Journal of Forensic Science in 2003 investigated the effect of a stun gun on the human body. 'Cutaneous current marks due to a stun gun injury' were examined on a 61-year-old man who died after having been tortured with a stun gun during a robbery. A taser would appear then to serve well as an instrument of torture. However, it also seems they can leave marks. 'At autopsy two reddish, dot-like lesions were found on the chest, and histological examination revealed electric current-related changes.' On the other hand, The Independent newspaper writes of 'the issue that can manifest even with proper training; That problem is torture. By design, these weapons leave few or no marks. Those who oversee the police have a difficult time determining if they were used properly or improperly. In essence, the weapons can evade detection.' So, we have conflicting opinion here; torture by means of a taser can either leave marks, or sinisterly not leave any. Of course, that's not to suggest a law enforcement officer attacked Henry McCabe or that he was being tasered at all. It's just a search for possible answers. Very interestingly, in this video of Police officers being tasered for part of their training, https://www.youtube.com/watch?v=UKRw4UPzPXs, the sounds that one policeman makes as the taser makes contact with his skin, sounds remarkably similar and indeed just as blood-curdling as Henry's screams that night, and just as non-human too. Like it is coming from a monster of our worst imaginations. On the internet, theories have ranged from; "Henry was attacked by bigfoot," to "Henry was being abducted by aliens," and that the noises were coming from the monsters or aliens themselves; not Henry. Some think that Henry was in a preternatural battle for his life that night. Yet, Henry drowned, according to his autopsy report.

Was Henry being drowned? Was he being waterboarded by an assailant that somehow managed not to capture any sounds of splashing or water? Or could Henry have been tortured elsewhere then taken to the water? How could a torturer or killer leave no marks? A highly-trained assassin? - skilled in the fine art of inflicting pain through pressure points or such like, using his fingers as weapons and leaving only internal injuries? Yet Henry was a simple family man, wasn't he? He had no known enemies and lived a lifestyle that did not beget foes. Henry was known as an advocate for the oppressed, and passionate about human rights, yet he was only known for this in his immediate family and friends and local community.

"Henry likes intelligent discussions," his wife Kareen said. His Facebook tribute page, formerly called 'Find Henry' says, 'One of Henry's favourite things to do was listen to 'Intelligence Squared' debates.' Newspaper Reports from his memorial service noted, 'He was easy-going, liked politics, and had an open, intellectual mind for understanding local and international issues. Henry asked, "What is justice?" and how it can be achieved?'

Henry was not known nationally or globally for his advocacy for minority voices and certainly, he did not seem outspoken enough to attract a political assassination! A visiting hitman from Liberia, Africa, sent to take him out, for some unknown reason perhaps? Yet surely that is far too dramatic? As an auditor, maybe he found something he should not have? But he was not a senior figure in auditing. There was nothing in his daily work activities that would have drawn enemies to him or led to him uncovering some huge conspiracy or cover-up, was there? He was not known to have any enemies at work either; no jealous rivals or competitors, at least as far as the police know, and remarks made by his boss and co-workers show no evidence of anything like that at all. He was a well-liked colleague. On his Facebook page, it says, 'He was generous to a fault and treated everyone he met as though he'd known them forever.' At work, he would offer his lunch to others. His family said, 'He used to say, "You can't stop the shinning." He shone bright,' they said.

Minnesota's Spokesman Reporter said, 'Deputy Commissioner of Minnesota Revenue Department, Ryan Church said McCabe touched many staff members. "It's really striking the impact Henry had. If you're greeted by Henry in the morning, you are greeted by an unforgettable smile. People just liked to hang out with Henry – it was Henry's magnetism and he really cares about people. We miss him." Kareen said, "If only Henry could see the number of people that came out to look for him and show their love for him, he would be overwhelmed."

Maybe Henry, walking home alone, was making those strange, disturbing noises because he was simply intoxicated and cold? Maybe it was like the sounds a person makes when they're freezing cold and they go 'Brrrrrrrr' with their lips as they shudder and shiver? Maybe he was cold, a little drunk, a little lost, and he walked 6 miles until he stopped at the creek. Maybe he fell in? Maybe it was just the sort of noises you would make on a dark night in late autumn when you find yourself suddenly falling into freezing water in the middle of nowhere? Although would you scream and beg and growl too, for several minutes? Did he stumble into the creek unknowingly, sink into the water, and find himself unable to get back out to land? Was he going into cold-water shock?

According to the State Department of Natural Resources, water robs body heat 25 times faster than cold air. Lisa Dugan, DNR's boat and water safety outreach coordinator says "Falling in cold water can bring muscle cramping and incapacitate people in seconds." Is this why his voice and words were so strange, so disjointed, so interspersed with guttural sounds? Was the cold water affecting his motor skills, especially combined with the amount of alcohol his friends say he had consumed? Did mental reasoning and speech become muddled, unclear, and this was why he left a riddled, garbled message? Yet his screams lasted for so long, and there were no sounds of water on the recording.

Could Henry have taken drugs perhaps, willingly or unwillingly? Was he hallucinating? Were his sensory skills all over the place? Did someone drug Henry, for nefarious purposes, and then watch him drown? Or, if Henry was alone, could it have been Henry's own voice telling himself to "Stop it?" Was he trying to get a grip on himself, trying to pull himself together and get himself out of there? As he walked through that woodland by the creek, could he even have thought someone was attacking him as he fought his way through the trees and bushes in the dark? Did a tap on the shoulder from a tree branch, or a scratch on the arm from a twig feel to Henry like the fingers of a pursuer, or the limbs of an animated monster? Did he start running, fleeing in panic, and fall into the water? And yet, there were no scratches on Henry. How was it possible that his body had no marks on it, given the location in which he was found? His wife thought he said he had been shot. Perhaps someone really was shooting at him. Was Henry hiding in the woods when he accidentally phoned his wife? Did he believe it was inevitable that he would die that night? Was it the horror of that realization that made him scream and howl? Yet the sounds he made were so visceral, so palpable, that it sounded like the worst physical pain imaginable….

Why did he say, "They are afraid?" What did he mean? What was it that made Henry howl and scream so unrelentingly that night?

Chapter Eighteen:

What happened to David Plunkett?

On Saturday the 17th of April 2005, 21-year-old David Plunkett was attending the Budweiser Music Event with a friend at the Daytona Racetrack in Trafford Park, just outside Manchester City Centre in Northern England. In the early hours of the following morning, David's parents received a phone call from David's friend, asking them if David was home. David's mother said he was not. David's friend explained that they'd been at the music event together but that David had been "kicked out" of the venue for allegedly being intoxicated. Mrs. Plunkett reassured David's friend she would call her son and find out where he was. When her son answered his mobile phone, at first, she heard only silence and what sounded like her son walking somewhere very quiet. Then, a few moments later David suddenly began to howl. His mother described it as a horrifying sound. "It was unearthly," she said. "I couldn't get through to him. He couldn't talk. He couldn't tell me where he was. A good 7-8 minutes into the call there was suddenly this ghastly screaming. I started crying." His mother said later that she can only believe her son saw something so terrifying, he could only scream.

Unable to get her son to listen to her, she passed the phone to her husband. Neither of his parents could get David to tell them where he was, or what was happening to him. David's father says, "I raised my voice to get him to snap out of it but I couldn't get through to him. He couldn't talk. We couldn't help him. Then there was total silence."

While Mr Plunkett stayed on the line with their son, Mrs. Plunkett called the police on their landline phone. The police tried to talk to David too but they got no response either.

"I took a very distressing 999 call," said the police operator. "He was in a distressed state but his parents couldn't hear anything other than his screaming. I stayed on with them for well over an hour, trying to provide assistance for them and him. The incident haunts me still." Three weeks later, David Plunkett's body was found in the Manchester Ship Canal, which runs through the City Centre.

Police later traced his phone to a location two miles outside the city and in an area David had no reason to be heading to. In fact, it was a spot he wouldn't have even known about. It led no-where. It was a dead-end, and it was not near his home. His phone was found on the path beside the canal, almost as though it had been placed carefully on the ground. His glasses were found beside the phone, undamaged, and again it was as if they had been calmly, carefully placed on the ground. The official ruling on David's death was that it was "Accidental," with the likely cause of death being "Drowning." To his parents however, this didn't make sense and they didn't believe his death was investigated as fully as it should have been. A former police detective from Scotland Yard was hired to investigate David's death some years later for a TV documentary. What the detective couldn't understand was why David would have gone to that location voluntarily. The route to the canal where David was said to have entered the water was down a small dark alley that appeared to be a dead-end. The detective also couldn't fathom how the Coroner and the police had established that David must have fallen into the water accidentally, when on order to have done that, he would have had to climb a very high fence first. The police said he had slipped down the embankment and into the water and that was why he had screamed. But David screamed continuously, for a very long time, as his parents could testify to. He screamed for far longer than it would have taken him to slip under the water and drown. Also, if he had fallen into the water, disregarding for a moment the very high fence he needed to climb first and then carefully take off his glasses and place them on the ground alongside his mobile phone; why didn't his parents hear any splashes of water as he fell in and struggled to stay afloat? Besides which, David wasn't calm that night; he was hysterical.

His mother, a former school head teacher said, "It is not a case of 'Young man drinks too much, falls in canal.'

Someone is responsible for his death and the version of events that have been given are simply not adding up, and the case leaves many more questions than answers. He could have been attacked, he could have had his drink spiked, anything.."

The police dispatcher from that night resigned, haunted by the hour-long sounds of David screaming.

What happened to David Plunkett that night? What did he see that made him scream so uncontrollably, and for so long?

Chapter Nineteen:

The Boy in the Red Dress

In November 2009, in the middle of the night in a rural province in China, Mrs. Gu Denghui is having a disturbing dream. In her dream she sees a tall, thin man wearing a suit. He is walking through the old village where she and her family used to live and where they still owned an abandoned house. He is carrying a bag of some kind and she watches as he approaches their old house. She cannot see his face as he wears a hat like a trilby. It hides his face, but as he approaches the back door to their house he stops, and she catches a glimpse of his mouth. It forms a wide smile. There is something very sinister about this man. He is carrying a package of some kind.

Mrs. Denghui's dream disturbed her so much that she told her husband about it the next morning and explained what she had seen. She urged her husband to go to their old house to see if anything had happened there. Her husband brushed it off, telling her it was just a dream.

Meanwhile, their 13-year-old son, Zhijun Kuang, is away at Boarding School. When he is not in lessons, he is happy reading his favourite book, 'Strange Tales from a Lonely Studio.' It's a famous Chinese book of ghost stories written way back in 1740.

The following day, Mrs. Denghui continued to tell her husband Kuang Jilu, a 54-year-old migrant farm worker, that he must go to their old home, and so finally he gave in, and he told her he would go and take a look, just to placate her. They lived in downtown Chongqing, where they worked, and so after work had ended that day, Mr. Jilu headed off to the old family home in the village of Shuangxing in the Banan District.

As he arrived in the small village, he met an elderly woman who was their old neighbour there. She stopped him and told him that she had seen a tall stranger in the village wearing a suit and a hat and carrying a bag. She said he had wandered through the village until he came to Mr. Jilu's old house, whereupon he walked around to the back of the house. She said she did not know who he was because the hat he was wearing hid his face. Mr. Jilu found himself becoming increasingly unsettled as he made small talk with his elderly neighbour, and he felt very anxious now to get to his old home. He quickly bid her 'goodbye' and walked off hurriedly. As he put his key in the front door, he found that the door would not open. Puzzled, he walked around to a side door, but again the same thing happened and the door would not budge. There was one more door he could try, at the back of the house, but this door had been boarded up for months, with planks of wood nailed across it and steel bar, which he had placed there to prevent anyone breaking into their empty property. He walked

around to the back of the house, and as he approached the back door, he was startled to discover that the steel bar was now lying on the ground and the thick planks of wood lay beside it. The door was open a few inches. With nervous trepidation and a terrible sense of unease, Mr. Jilu pushed open the door and entered. The lights were on inside the house and the place looked dishevelled, but what drew his eye almost immediately was the horrifying sight in front of him. The body of his son was hanging by a rope from a wooden roof beam. He was hanging by his hands, which had been bound tightly together. His feet had also been bound. His whole body had been tied tightly by ropes, and a large heavy scale hung down between his feet. On the scale was the number 1. His son was wearing a red dress. Mr. Jilu rushed to release his son from the ropes, but it was too late – his body was already cold. Grief sunk the father to his knees as he cried out for his boy.

In time, the police arrived. They saw no footprints and no sign of a struggle. Nothing had been stolen. There was 32.5 yuan on the floor. The boy's school text books lay scattered on the floor. His school bag, watch and mobile phone, along with some compact discs were also there. There were two packs of instant noodles, one of which had been eaten. How long had the boy been hanging there? His father later said, "His mobile phone was broken a few days ago so I couldn't contact him." Mr. Jilu also added that on the day of the discovery of his son's body, he had gone to send money to his son, who attended boarding school. His parents had naturally believed that their son had been at the boarding School; however, it transpired that the entire school had been closed after an outbreak of influenza, and the school had believed that their son had returned home like all the other children. The boy had never arrived home however; and his parents had no idea he was missing for four days. His father said, "If it wasn't for my wife who had a dream that someone entered the old house in the countryside then my son's body may have rotted and no-one would know."

The police would soon say that there had been no intruder. On December the 3rd, the police released a report that said the boy's death was 'an accident.' His father applied for a reconsideration – he could not accept this determination. Ten days later, on December the 11th, the police told him that after careful consideration and re-investigation, there was "no clue of murder or suicide," and that their original determination stood.

The boy's autopsy revealed that the marks from the ropes on 'the thighs, hands and bare feet are extremely deep.' From looking at the crime scene photos of his body hanging there, which are sadly available on the internet, they show that the boy had deep, tight lines of rope cutting into his legs. His whole body had been tied tightly by the ropes, and a large heavy scale was hung as a weight between his feet. His hands were tied and hung on the wooden beam that was part of the roof inside the house. There were 12 intricate knots tied on his hands and feet. How could the boy have done this to himself? His parents said he had no history of learning how to tie knots. On the boy's forehead was a tiny pinhole. Other than that, he had no wounds, apart from the savage impressions into his skin, caused by the tightness of the ropes. His feet were a few centimetres off the ground. A bench beside him was overturned. On the wooden back door, the word "Kill" was written, along with the word "King." King of the Kill? A cross had also been drawn, although his father thought this could have been there prior to his son being killed. Chinese news site 原文網址 reported that the Banan District Criminal Investigation Team had arrived at the scene not long after the boy's discovery, and shortly after this, the medical examiner also arrived. They reported that, 'Jilu said the forensic doctor told him the initial judgement was that his son had died within the last 48 hours – on November 3rd or 4th. He had many deep marks but the boy had almost no actual trauma.' If he had no trauma, how did he die?

The father told reporters that detectives in charge of the criminal investigation told him that neither the district bureau nor the city bureau could explain the phenomenon that occurred. The father said police at the scene took off the boy's red dress. Underneath the dress was a woman's bathing suit. The dress and the bathing suit did not belong to the boy. The swimsuit had been padded with black cloth, which made it look like the boy had breasts. The police said the boy must have been playing a game. His father responded; "What kind of game would make my son put on a swim suit and skirt, tie himself up by his hands and feet and hang himself from the roof?" The way the ropes were tied looked very professional, and how could the boy have hanged himself from the beam if his hands were intricately bound together with many knots? And why would he stick a pin into his forehead?

In China, people could not understand this. Had something been pinned to his forehead, like a note, or a playing card? Yet, if this had been done by someone else, why were there no signs of a struggle, no serious injuries or wounds? Had the boy been drugged? Or, had harm been threatened to him, or his family, if he did not comply? The boy's father said that the red dress looked like one his niece owned, although it did not seem to be hers. No-one could find the identity of the person who owned the woman's bathing suit, that the boy had worn under his dress. Mr. Jilu and the boy's mother could not understand why he was wearing a dress. As far as they were aware, their son had not shown any previous indications of being a cross-dresser or transvestite; besides which, he was just 13 years old. Disbelief was also expressed among the locals too. However, there was the suggestion by those in authority, as well as those prone to gossip, that the boy must have been experimenting with his sexuality, and that he had stuffed paper into the swimsuit to give himself breasts. Newspapers in China reported, 'Jilu said that his son in the last few days did not display any abnormal behaviour.' At Dongquan Middle school, his 7th grade teacher told reporters, "Zhai did not like to talk, he was honest and his grades were lower in the class, but his behaviour was normal." Neighbours including Wang Lunqin told reporters that the family are "Very honest friendly people, who never had disputes with others. Zhizhi is usually less talkative with people, shy. He never takes the initiative to speak to people. I have never seen him in clothing like that in the past." 70-year-old neighbour, Deng Xianbi said the boy, "Is usually playful and not bad, and his mother and father are honest and never argue. It is not believed that he had the quirk to wear girls' clothes." Some of the school boys at his boarding school said he very much liked to read 'Strange Tales from a Lonely Studio'. Had he been acting-out a scene from his favourite book?

One theory put forward by the Chinese media was that the boy's mother's first husband and their eldest son might have conspired to kill the boy in revenge over some sort of dispute. One newspaper in China quoted Mr. Jilu as saying, "The assassinator, the killer, is the former husband of Denghui and their son, whose custody after divorce was given to the child's father." The boy's mother accused her ex-husband of taking her son and 'hiding him' – but police made it clear; 'They reject this possibility.' The police did question both the ex-husband and the son, but both of them had water-tight alibis.

'The boy, Kuang Zhijun, was definitely determined to have been killed accidentally,' the Chongqing Morning Post reported. His parents, and many others however, disagreed emphatically that this had in no way been 'an accident.' The boy would never have done something this strange, and nor was it even physically possible. The police, in growing frustration, made the statement that the death had occurred while the boy was playing some kind of "superstitious" game, and closed the investigation. But where did the red dress and bathing suit come from? And how could he have tied himself up with such intricate knots?

Chinese occultists offered another theory; that the death had been a rare, once in a century ritual. The boy had died aged 13 years and 13 days. The paraphernalia of the scale, the dress, the wood; these were the five elements. The wood beam represented wood. The bathing suit represented water. The red dress represented fire. This was ancient Taoist sorcery, they said. An individual or a sect had killed the boy in order to "raise him as a ghost." The pinhole in his forehead signified the separation of the soul from the body, and the weight hanging from his feet signified keeping his soul on earth, while the red dress representing fire, bound his soul to the killer. 'This is the death method that will break up the soul and it will never pass. The soul is forever doomed to the earth realm. And, the killer seems to have wanted to steal this soul. The split needle (the pinhole), the lock of the soul, are exclusive spells of Maoshan,' Occultists proposed. This 'Ghost keeping' can be used to keep 'Spiritual servants; as soldiers of the netherworld.' As for the pinhole, Chinese occultist Netizens explains, "According to the records of Mashan Dao," which is an ancient Taoist sorcery, "The needle should be soaked with corpse oil for 981 days. The boy was killed to be raised as a ghost." Says reporter Yuánwén Wǎngzhǐ, "The killer will be familiar with the date of birth of the child. They will use the red clothes to lock the soul. The person is likely to be an elder and an expert in ritualistic magic, and the purpose was to extend their own life. The person to be dealt with must be powerful and unusual, and very sophisticated. The planner of this case is likely a high-powered person. It seems that the purpose of the murderer is not to hurt the soul but to take the soul," and, "to raise a ghost. The soul needle is inserted from the top of the head. The pin is to lock the soul first, then vent the soul, and finally to take the soul. The police must know this is a bad thing. If the police want to break this case it is impossible without the help from metaphysics – but the thing is, I am afraid that people who are this good at spells are afraid to intervene. There are very few people who could do this."

'Two days after the death of Kuang Zhijun,' says China's Online Edition, 'An 18-year-old approached the boy's father and told him he had recently seen a man circling in the neighbourhood near the dilapidated house. The witness said he was dragging a sack behind him. He did not however see his face because of the hat he wore, just as the tall stranger had done in Denghui's dream.'

Who was this mysterious man?

Chapter Twenty:

The Lipstick on the Dead

In 1997, in the Cumbrian Lake District of England, a father and son were travelling in their car when they went missing. Mr. John Lee and his son Connor, 14, had been visiting relatives in the area, but had not been seen since they left. It was to be a fortnight before their bodies were found near Lake Windermere. Their car had crashed and flipped them upside down. Neither of them survived the accident.

It could not be determined what had caused their car to go upside down as it careered off the road into a meadow; however, that was not the biggest part of the mystery. There was a macabre twist to their sad demise. On the teenage boy's face, very close to the corner of his mouth, there was a red lipstick mark, which according to the medical examiner had been put there at least 10 days after the car crash. This would mean that the lipstick mark had appeared after the boy was dead. No-one knows how that lipstick mark got there. Forensic tests undertaken on the lipstick concluded that it was a brand of lipstick most popular among girls in their early teens back then in the nineties.

The bodies of the son and his father were not discovered for two weeks, because their car had come to rest in a wooded part of a meadow and had been thereby hidden from passing view.

When reporter Clive Rupertson covered the strange mystery back then, it seems that an extensive search had been carried out for the missing car and its passengers, and yet strangely their car had not been found. Police officers who attended the scene after their car was discovered, expressed their bafflement at both the re-appearance of the car, and more oddly, at how the lipstick mark could have come to be on the face of the boy. To the police, this was a "highly unusual" case, and they put out an appeal to the general public for any information.

Could someone else have been at the scene at the time of the accident, and tried to comfort the dying boy? But surely, they would have called an ambulance, or the police? Had someone come across the car and their bodies, and in morbid sympathy, left a kiss on the dead boy's mouth? Had a group of youths been out one night and stumbled across the crash and carried out a ghoulish dare? Had a relative who he and his father had been visiting, kissed the boy 'goodbye' on the mouth before they left? And yet, the medical examiner said the lipstick was put on the boy approximately 10 days after they crashed. Who kissed the dead boy?

Chapter Twenty-One:

The curious case of Christopher Case

In April 1991, Christopher Case was Director of Programming for Muzak, the Company responsible for introducing elevator music and department store jingles. As a teenager, Christopher had been passionate about music. He grew up in Richmond, Virginia, and was known by all his friends and family for his love of music as well as for being a fitness fanatic. He'd been a DJ back then and had often preferred listening to music than socializing and going out at night.

The worst anyone could say about him was that he was sometimes a bit of a loner. A good friend from his DJ days in Richmond, Sammye Saddo said, "One of the reason's I get emotional about it is because he was my friend and I loved him, and I didn't like the way he died. He would travel around the world with his job, so he didn't date much but women liked him. He was the kind of guy you could rely on – everybody's friend."

Fast forward to the night he died and Christopher had almost resigned himself to his fate. He had accepted that his death would most likely come. He felt that he simply would not be able to stop it, and although he put up a fight, his fears were confirmed. He did not make it through the night. He was found clothed in a kneeling position, dead, surrounded by crosses and crucifixes and salt. The candles he had lit had burned-down. He had no wounds. Soft religious music was still playing in the background. He had prepared himself for a strange battle, and he had lost.

One of the reporters who covered his story back in 1991 was Lewis Course for the Seattle Times, who said, "What intrigued me was the fact that from everything I knew from what I'd been told about it, he was pretty level-headed." Nobody who knew him could understand the week in the summer of '91 that ended in his death.

It all began when he'd gone on a business trip to San Francisco. While there, a male business friend had introduced him to a woman who was importing rare music from Egypt. She had some information on ancient Egyptian music, he told Christopher, and of course, music was Chris's life, so he was very interested in this, but Christopher would later say there was something very strange about the dark-haired woman he met. She had an intensity about her, he said. It was also obvious to Christopher that she wanted to start a relationship with him. She was older than he was, and she was, in his opinion, quickly enamoured of him, and he didn't like that at all. He had no interest in her whatsoever, other than the ancient Egyptian music she knew so much about.

The second time they met, to continue discussing the music, was in a restaurant. She came on even stronger to Christopher that night, he later told his close friends, and he said he pulled away from her, telling her it was time they left. This greatly angered her, and she uttered something strange to him, he said. She said that he would be very sorry. She told him she was going to put a curse on him.

A few days later, Christopher returned home from his business trip, and for a time everything was normal. He dismissed the incident from his mind, the way most rational people would. He mentioned it to his friend Sammye, but he didn't sound alarmed when he first told her, she said. He said, this lady I met, she said she's a witch, and Sammye said she told him, "Just bless her and go on about your business." This was the first of three calls he made to his close friend Sammye, and the calls would become increasingly worse, until the night of Wednesday 17th April 1990 when he would find himself in a mortal battle for his life.

It had been less than a week since his meeting with this mystery woman. He had not heard from her again after leaving San Francisco; yet, "It seemed that his encounters with her were beginning to play on his mind," said Sammye, "And it was horrible. I wish someone could hear what I heard in his voice, and what he said. It was a living hell. It's my understanding that he would try to sleep but he had gotten to the point that he was not sleeping."

A couple of days after returning from his trip, Christopher visited a religious book store called Evangeline Inc, not far from his apartment. The Store manager, Rodney Higuchi took particular notice of Christopher as he browsed the store. Christopher asked Higuchi where the Crosses were. "Then I saw him collect quite a few in his hands, so I asked him what he was going to be using them for and he mentioned that he was battling some supernatural forces and he wanted them for protection. He wanted to know if they had been blessed with holy water."

Christopher told the Store manager, "I just don't know what to do now. I can't sleep." Christopher left the Store and returned to his apartment. He placed the crosses and crucifixes in every room and spread salt in all the corners.

Later that day, he phoned his friend Sammye again. "It's like they're putting thoughts in my head before I can even think them," he told her. "They've attacked me in the middle of the night." He told her had woken up to find small cuts on his fingers. He was terrified. He hadn't shown up for work in two days. He sat in his apartment and wrote notes on methods of combating evil spirits. He told his worried friends that he believed the curse was taking hold of him. That night, he became so terrified that he felt he could not remain in his apartment. He left and checked into a hotel nearby.

When he returned to his apartment the following day, he wrote more notes on rituals he could do to fight the powers of darkness that were so violently besieging him. He lined the base of each wall with more salt, and he fashioned a geometric pattern in salt at the front door. He spread copious amounts of salt in large piles in every corner of the rooms.

Then returned to the spiritual Bookstore Store once more. This time, the Bookstore owner felt that he was seeing a changed man. Mr Higuchi said, "When he first came in, he wasn't very agitated, and nothing looked out of the ordinary. When he came in the second time, he looked exhausted and worn out, and then I realized that it was affecting him more than just mentally. I mean, it was a physical thing he was going through. When I talked with him on that Wednesday morning, my feeling was he was ready to die, because he said to me; "You know, I can die from this."

Shortly after 10 p.m. that night, Sammye called the Seattle police with grave concerns that Christopher had not answered her calls all day. Homicide Detective Larry Peterson King Kelly said police initially received information to warrant a welfare check at Christopher's apartment prior to the night of his death. When the police arrived at his apartment, they found his apartment door locked and received no response from knocking on his door. They noticed a line of salt outside his front door. They later said they felt they had no reason to break down his door however, as they did not think the welfare call was an emergency. Neighbours would later tell the homicide detectives that Christopher Case was a very private man.

After Christopher's second trip to the Bookstore, it later transpired that he also visited a Priest, apparently in a desperate state. Father James Mallahan later told the TV show The Extraordinary, that he had been disturbed by Christopher's condition. He could tell Christopher Case was scared to death and that his terror was greatly affecting his physical condition as well as his mind. The Priest said Chase asked him for advice on how to combat supernatural forces. He was in great fear that he was going to be killed, Christopher told him.

That evening, Sammye returned home to find an ansaphone message on her phone from Christopher. It was the last time she heard his voice. "Oh well," he said, "They just about got me." The most chilling aspect of the message, she said, was his total acceptance of his fate. The next day, all her calls to him went unanswered. At 3.38 pm that afternoon, the police entered his apartment. It was a mess. There were scribbled notes everywhere. The floor was littered with his writing and covered with piles of salt.

"I heard religious music playing on the radio from the living room," said the homicide detective. A flicker of light came through the bathroom doorway. As the detectives entered the bathroom, they came across the final frozen moment of Christopher Case's life. The candles had burned down. He was kneeling, as though in prayer. "I saw the victim slumped over on his knees with his head resting on the edge of the tub, left of the faucet."

He was in the bathtub, fully clothed. "A trickle of cold water ran from the tap. He was still wearing his glasses." He had died sometime during the night. The Seattle coroner officially ruled the cause of death as cardiac arrest; but those who knew him, especially during the final week of his life, believed there was a lot more to his demise.

'Heart Failure Killed Man Who Feared `Curse,' wrote the local Newspaper. The cause of death was acute myocarditis, said Rich Garner, a medical investigator with the King County Medical Examiner's office. Myocarditis is an inflammation of the heart muscle.

The Seattle Times wrote; 'Mystery Death of North Kingston Man whose body was found surrounded by occult symbols. There was no evidence of foul play, but the presence of crucifixes and piles of salt throughout the apartment have baffled investigators. Kings County Police Major Jackson said the salt and other objects at the scene have some significance in self-protection against demons or evil spirits.'

King County Police Major Jackson Beard said, "At this point, this is a suspicious death; something that needs to be explained." But he added, "I don't believe there was any foul play – this could be suicide or natural death or there was something else going on here."

He said he was waiting on toxicology results. They later came back clean. Christopher didn't smoke, hardly drank and did not take drugs. Sammye said she had known Christopher for 10 years and that he had always been stable; until a week earlier. "People are trying to do things to me," he told her in the first phone call. He left the same message with another close female friend too. "He was frantic," said Sammye.

On April the 14th, the first of three phone calls, Christopher called her claiming to be up all-night hearing whispering voices that he could not find the source of. He said he felt as though he was being watched and he said he could see moving shadows in the apartment. He was terrified.

"I believe he died of fright," said Sammye. He had lit the candles, thrown more salt, and climbed into the bath tub fully dressed, to try to survive until morning. He'd never been under the supervision of a Doctor for heart inflammation. He was a fitness fanatic and lived a clean, healthy lifestyle. He'd never been off work ill before. Did Christopher Case scare himself to death? Did an underlying heart inflammation happen to kill him in the exact week that he believed he would die? Or did a curse really end his life….? "I only have one week to live," he'd told his friends. "They're after me. I am very, very afraid," he had said.

Chapter Twenty-Two:

The tale of Jacob Mutton

In a little corner of the reading room of the Oxford's Bodleian Library, a former assistant Police Commander Brian Langston was to discover an incredible pamphlet from a century gone-by. Langston, now a researcher of mystery, crime and the paranormal, would discover that inside the pamphlet was an incredible tale from the late 17th century of a young boy living in Cornwall, who one night was apparently inexplicably transported a distance of 30 miles 'by an unknown force.'

The young boy in question was called Jacob Mutton, and he was a servant employed by the Rector of Cardinham, William Hicks, who lived on Bodmin Moor in Cornwall. Bodmin Moor is in England's rugged southwestern tip and a designated Area of Outstanding Natural Beauty. It's a wild, rugged and bleak yet beautiful heather-covered granite moorland of 208 square kilometres. Here the servant boy Jacob Mutton lived, and he was described as an honest and hard-working employee by the Rector and all others who knew him. The event in question occurred sometime after 8 pm on Sunday the 8th May 1687. Jacob had just taken himself off to bed in the Rectory. He shared a bedroom with another servant boy, who was at the time already in bed.

Jacob would later explain that as he began to get undressed for bed, he started to hear a voice which he described as "hollow," and this voice was saying, "So hoe, so hoe, so hoe." It sounded as though the voice was coming from a nearby room, and the servant boy went off to investigate. In this other room, he could hear the voice again, but it sounded as if it was coming from outside the window. He approached the window and peered out of it, but he could see nothing in the dark outside. The last memory he had was of looking out the window, until the following morning when he was found lying unconscious in a countryside lane by folks travelling to market at Stratton Fair.

As they roused him, he appeared to be completely baffled about what he was doing lying in the country lane, in a spot he did not recognise at all. He was approximately 4 miles from the town of Bude and 30 miles from his home at the Rectory. The travelling group couldn't just leave him there all alone and confused, and so they took him with them to the market Fair. Once the Fair was over, the group set him on the right road to make his way back home, now a distance of 20 miles from the Rectory. He was eventually discovered by other travellers on the road and taken to spend the night in the village of Camelford.

The following morning, he continued his journey on foot alone and eventually he arrived back home at the Rectory the following day, having walked all night to get home. Fortunately, he had made it home in one piece and physically looked no worse the wear for it. However, the Rector noticed that his demeanour appeared changed. He was very quiet, and he appeared sad. This was not the usual behaviour of this normally cheerful boy. Mind you, he had just walked thirty miles! But this demeanour continued as the days passed.

The Rector of course was concerned about where Jacob had been all this time, and when he asked his servant boy about this, all Jacob could explain was that 'the Tall man' had taken him 'Over hedges...without weariness or hurt,' but he could not say what had happened to his companion, 'the Tall man.'

"There the story ends," says Brian Langston. "The brevity of the account is fascinating, frustrating and leaves many unanswered questions."

Cornish folklorist Sue Field says, 'Some say he was abducted by aliens and thrown out of their flying saucer on the other side of Cornwall when they couldn't work out what to do with him. Some say teleportation, and he had flown high above the woods and bogs, tors and moors until he came to Stratton. But some of us know that Cornwall is a land of giants, and that Bevill Grenville, the Kings General, had a giant for a servant, named Anthony Payne. In the year of Jacob's journey Anthony Payne was an old, old giant and needed a servant of his own to care for him. Giants look after their own, and rumour had it that a giant,

Soho, went looking for a servant for Payne. He peered in many attic windows until he spotted Jacob, and thought he would do, so he grabbed him through the window bar and strode over the Moor....'

Who really was the mysterious stranger "The Tall Man?" and what did he want with Jacob?

Chapter Twenty-Three:

The last haunting photo

A haunting last photo is all that his parents are left with. The photo is a close-up shot of his face, set against a bleak, dark landscape. He is alone, we think. He is lost, we believe, and he is very afraid. How he vanished has never been solved. He was a boy scout aged 12, and he vanished into thin air. He was with his scout group on a hike. There one minute, gone the next.

It was July the 19th 1991, and 12-year-old Jared Negrete was on his first overnight camping trip in the San Gorgorio wilderness in the South-Eastern part of the San Bernardino National Forest of California. It is an area the LA Times calls, 'A breath-taking bramble of rocky crags, sandy switchbacks, and dozens of trails, many of which meander to nowhere.'

After Jared disappeared, a 19-day search for him found only his camera with that last haunting photo, and some discarded candy wrappers. How could he vanish in the middle of the wilderness? There was no road to leave by, no transport out of there; no route out, apart from a very long hike.

"The hardest part is at night, knowing he's out there by himself in the wilderness," said Linda Negrete, his mother, who called out to her son over a public address system for days after he vanished, from a helicopter circling the search area.

'Searchers find camera belonging to Jared,' wrote Associated Press. 'Camera found as they followed footprints they believed were made by the missing boy. The film in the 5 foot 2, 150 lb boy's camera was developed, but proved to be of no use to searchers.' All it had was an eerie close-up of his face. The photo looked as though it had been taken after night had fallen. 'A roll of film in the camera showed at least 7 photos officials believe were taken after Jared was separated from his scout troop. The picture was apparently taken by holding the camera out at arm's length.' That is certainly one explanation, and probably the correct one, but what if it had been an abductor taking this photo of Jared, terrified and helpless; a photograph taken as a taunt and then his camera dropped to the ground, left to be found and his parents to see, as a sick joke, goading them?

This would not be unique. Think of the terribly evil 'Truck Stop Killer' Robert Ben Rhoades, who made his abducted young female victim put on a black dress he had purchased for her, and be photographed just moments before he killed her. The visceral terror in her eyes has been captured for eternity and spread across the internet for millions to see. Is that what happened to Jared? And yet, he was in the middle of the wilderness. And, wouldn't his kidnapper's footprints have been found there in the dusty ground? Tracker dogs and thousands of searchers on foot and on horseback narrowed in on a 4-square mile radius around the site where his camera had been found. On August the 9th, it was reported, 'Shoe prints were found at around 10,000 feet,' and it was believed that these footprints could be Jared's. Not far from the boy's camera, a few candy wrappers had been found, and an indentation in the ground near his footprints, that searchers said looked like the boy had slid approximately 9 feet down a small slope on his bottom. Where he went from there, is impossible to say; for very oddly, no footprints were found leading away in any direction.

Jared had last been seen hiking on the Vivian Trail. His Kodak camera was found under a bush 200 feet off this trail. Nearly 7,000 rescuers and volunteers scoured the San Bernardino Mountains for 16 days using helicopters, dog teams, horses, infra-red devices; all without success in finding the missing boy. It would turn out to be the State's largest and most expensive missing person's search, involving thousands of man-hours. The Marines were brought in to help.

The boy scout group had begun their hiking trip at Camp Tahquitz, south of Big Bear Lake. Jared had set off on the hike with 12 other scouts to reach the 11,500-foot summit of the mountain. As the group got to within 500 feet from the summit however, Jared apparently become very tired and he started flagging behind the rest of the scouts. This didn't seem to have been noticed by the group themselves, but some hikers in the area noticed him, and they informed Jared's scout leader.

At this point, scout leader Dennis Knight told Jared to rest there and stay behind, while the remainder of the group continued on up to the summit. He said he told Jared they would be back shortly.

However, when Knight returned with the other scouts, Jared was no longer there. Shocked, the scout leader quickly told the boys to search the immediate vicinity for Jared. He couldn't imagine the boy could be far away; after all, the reason Jared had been left behind was because he had become tired, so the last thing anyone could have expected was that he would have taken off hiking by himself. That wouldn't have made any sense, but strangely, the scouts could see no sign of him on the trail nor anywhere around them.

The group hiked back along the trail they had come, back to their camp as fast as possible and then Knight hiked for 5 miles in the dark to fetch help. At around midnight he made first contact with park officials. The search began in the early hours.

It was not the middle of winter, it was July, and so temperatures were relatively mild, and the authorities said there was sufficient water in the area to enable Jared to survive for several days.

'Loss of Scout is unexplainable,' wrote AP News, 8 days into the search. Newspapers reported constantly with any updates as the search progressed into hours, then days. On the 9th day of the search, San Bernardino County Sheriff's Department reported on the discovery of the missing boy's camera.

All the evidence of the missing boy now seemed to be in a 1-mile radius: the camera, the candy wrappers, along with one set of footprints. But where did he go from there?

Said Tanya Cahill, Spokesperson for the Sheriff's department, "We have somebody's baby out here. We aren't going to quit searching."

The Newton Times of July the 29th 1991 reported, 'In the brutal terrain, infrared monitors were installed at a number of high points Saturday night in the hope of spotting the boy in the dark,' but, 'Only deer and other animals were detected by the monitors, said searchers.'

As the searches continued, Bishop Frank Barney of El Monde's Church of Jesus Christ of the Latter-Day Saints, who sponsored Jared's 538 scout troop, said, "He's young, and very shy, and a little overweight, and was allowed to get a little behind the others." Of course, many will blame the Scout leader, and these days, more than one leader would be expected to go with a group; but before we are too hard on the leader, Jared was only 500 feet away, and there really was no-where to go. So, who would have imagined the boy could simply vanish into thin air?

In all, the searchers covered a 120 square mile radius of the wilderness, comprising swathes of forest and jagged rocks.

"They're checking every creak and crevice - anywhere that a 12-year-old boy could go," said Deputy Sheriff Debra Donough. "We know Jared had still been alive when he took the last photos at dusk," Jared's uncle Harvey Beach told reporters.

"Jared always carried some goodies with him," another uncle, Leo Cotz said. Jared used to accompany him on shorter hikes. Among the searchers, nearly a dozen uncles and cousins gathered. His parents remained at home. They were too distraught to come to the wilderness where their boy was now lost. His mother could not bring herself to look at the last photo taken by her son.

Meanwhile, days turned into weeks. Sheriff Lenew said "Volunteers focus on an area of thick chaparral – it's very slow going up there." He said the lead tracker was following a trail through vegetation so thick that at times he was only able to cover as little as 150 feet per hour. Then the trail the tracker had been following seemingly simply stopped. Was this Jared's trail? And if so, how could his trail simply suddenly stop?

Still the searchers carried on. San Bernardino County Fire fighter Bill Garcia had already spent 18 hours a day on the search for Jared. He still held out hope. "There's plenty of water. There's fish in some of the creeks; with a little ingenuity, there are enough resources to live off. If he keeps his wits, he should be able to get by." Could he have drowned in one of the small creeks? Yet the dogs went in the creeks and they did not detect the boy's scent. The LA Times reported, 'Footprints have led nowhere.' How could this be? How did Jared simply vanish into thin air?

Jared's mother once said, "It's desperation, horror. No-one can comprehend it. But I know it. I have nothing. I don't even have a grave." Jared was never found. At the time of his disappearance, the Muncie Evening Press said, 'His mother clings to her memories of the last minutes she spent with her son. As he got out of the family car, he assured her he would be very careful. "He was so proud because he was going on his first boy scout's hike. He was with his friends, and I didn't want to embarrass him so I mouthed, "I love you" and "Be careful." He mouthed back, "I love you" and "I will." That's the last memory I have." She was never able to bring herself to look at the last photo of her son, taken alone in the darkness. Even cadaver dogs never found him. If he'd been abducted, there would have been two sets of footprints; but there weren't.

"You could see in the photo that he was very scared," Felipe Negrete, his father said.

What happened to Jared Ngrete?

Chapter Twenty-Four:

The puzzle of Charles Mccullar

Crater Lake National Park in Southern Oregon is one of the most scenic places in the world to visit, and it is famous for its lake of striking blue. The collapse of Mount Mazama almost 8,000 years ago from a volcano resulted in the formation of a caldera that now holds the Lake, at an elevation of 8,000 feet. It's the deepest body of freshwater in the United States. Surrounding the Lake are thick forests and hills. In the west of the Lake is Wizard Island, a conical cinder formed of pyroclastic fragments from the volcanic explosion.

On January the 29th 1975, 19-year-old Charles Mccullar left his home in Virginia and hitched rides to reach his friends in Oregon, where he intended to stay for a short vacation. During his stay, he planned to make his way to Crater Lake, taking with him his camera equipment to capture the breath-taking beauty of the lake and the forests there. He was a keen amateur photographer.

When he left his friends' house, he told them he would be back in two days, but he never returned. When it was realized he was missing, National Park Service Rangers and volunteers began to search for him. The search was not easy because of the weather conditions at the time. However, according to the Crater Lake Foundation, a massive ground and air search was conducted for McCullar at the direction of the young man's father, and in fact Mr. McCullar would go on to spend much of the summer camped at various locations in the National Park, searching in hope for his son. Thorough grid searches were carried out, lasting for weeks; but they found no sign of him. The Cascade Rescue Emergency Service teams searched the area extensively by snowmobile, skis, and hiking. They could find no tracks and no trace of McCullar. His father would go on to contact the FBI, his Congressman; anyone who might listen to his worries that his son was still out there, unfound.

Then, twenty months later, the local Newspaper reported, 'No trace of young McCullar is found until October 14th 1976,' and this is where things get weird. Hikers had come across a backpack and car keys lying on the ground near Bybee Creek. They took the items to the Park staff, who went to the area where the items had been found. It was almost thirteen miles from the trailhead where Mccullar had last been seen on the day he vanished. There had been seven and a half feet of new snow on the ground at the time of this disappearance. The snow was so thick and high that it would seem impossible McCullar could have travelled 13 miles on foot, off the trail, in snow that was taller than him. The location where he was found was well-off the trail. Surely, this was simply not possible?

As the Rangers searched the area where his car keys and backpack had been found, sadly they discovered McCullar's partial remains too. Much of his body was gone by now, because of the environment and because of natural predators. His jeans were still there. They were found unbuttoned. His coat was missing, his shirt was gone, and so too were his boots. Is it possible he had undressed as hypothermia set in? This often makes a person feel very hot when they are actually freezing cold; but if so, where did his coat go, and his boots? His expensive camera had disappeared too. Had he been robbed? Would a robber be out in snow taller than himself too?

If McCullar had somehow miraculously managed to travel 13 miles in the snow, then the question is; why would he even have done that? And even stranger was how had he left no tracks to follow? There should have been a long trail of footprints for the searchers to follow straight to his location, shouldn't there?

The second very strange thing was the odd condition of his skeleton. Some of the bones from his feet were found in his socks, but his jeans were completely empty of bones, except for the broken-off ends of his shin-bones, which were sticking up. Where had all his leg bones gone? And what had happened to him to make his shins snap off?

The rest of his bones were gone too, according to Charles "Butch" Farbee, Head of the Department of The Interior and responsible for the management and conservation of Federal Land. He said it was "As if he had melted away!" Says John D. Finn of Offbeat Oregon Magazine, "They never found his boots; just an empty pair of pants sitting on a log, with socks and foot-bones inside."

The crown of McCullar's skull was found along with a lower jawbone, about 10 feet away from his broken-off shin bones. A Klamath Falls pathologist advised that the teeth in the lower jaw bone and the skull matched perfectly with McCullar's dental chart. The pathologist said he saw no indication of damage to the skull that would indicate foul play.

Officers from the Oregon State Crime Lab were flown into the area by helicopter to conduct a more thorough search. The area where McCullar was found was described as a 'Remote, mountainous and rugged area.' How did he get into an area such as this? The theory the park rangers came up with was that McCullar must have been trying to cross a frozen creek, as it would have been the easiest path of travel, and that he had fallen in through broken ice and perished. But if so, how did his skeleton happen to end up sitting on a log in a "remote and rugged" area, and not in the creek? Could McCullar actually have been abducted on the hiking trail, or before he set out on his supposed 13-mile trek, and then his body taken back to the area sometime later and placed in this remote spot? For how else could he have reached it, when there had been snow taller than him when he'd set out? However, Oregon crime lab analysed samples of hair and clothing at the scene, and they determined that McCullar had died at that spot. He had not died or been killed elsewhere. They believed he died of exposure, and that there was no indication foul play. But how did McCullar's skeleton come to be sitting on a log? And what had snapped his shin bones off?

Another very strange story about Crater Lake comes from the 1940's, when a husband and wife, Mr and Mrs Cornelius were visiting. They were standing gazing out over the lake when suddenly Mrs Cornelius found herself watching in shock and disbelief as her husband took out his wallet, took off his watch, and handed them to her to hold. Then he sat himself down in the snow, pushed himself off a snow chute, and slid toward the lake at speed. He broke his leg in this inexplicable act, but he didn't let that stop him. He crawled to the shore of the lake, entered the water, and drowned himself. Of course, we do not have details on his mental state nor any problems he may have been facing in his life, but certainly it would appear a very odd thing to suddenly do. For the indigenous Native Americans, Crater Lake was always regarded as a sinister place. Legend has it that they would never look upon the lake; for to do so would be to fall under its spell and it would call you to it, luring you to your death.

Chapter Twenty-Five:

The Wax Men The Stick Men & The Mannequins

A man called Simon Howes, who is a nurse, wrote into a forum for the Fortean Times of a strange incident that happened to him back in 1982, in Essex, England. 'At Warley Hospital, Brentwood, I encountered a 'stick person' in the grounds of the Hospital as I was walking home one night. It lopped across the roadway having been seemingly pressed up against a wall. It stopped when it saw me and raised its arms in fright and quickly walked off into the undergrowth. It was very tall with very thin, extremely long arms and legs and a very small oval head. Totally black and no obvious clothing. I saw no face even though it emerged very near a streetlamp and so it was well illuminated. I was terrified and to this day, no-one believes me.'

If one were to think this an hallucination however, one might be wrong. In 2003, a man called Andy wrote into The Cauldron about an experience that happened to him when he was attending University in London and living 'in a leafy suburb called Brockley.' It was 'an experience for which I have no explanation. In the early hours of the morning I was walking back from a friend's house where another friend Sue and myself had spent the whole night talking and revising with a group of other people. I had drunk only tea all night and had consumed no drugs whatsoever. Dawn was just breaking as we turned onto my street. We were very tired and didn't say much to each other until I spotted a man walking up towards us on the same path, some distance away. I didn't think anything of it; in a city like London, people are up and about at all hours. He could have been a milkman, a refuse collector, a night-shift worker heading home.

We walked towards the man. He walked towards us. My home was between us. I began to feel uneasy. The word we coined later to describe its movement was 'lolloping' - a kind of up-down bouncy walk. I asked my friend: "See that man?"

"Yes," was the reply.

"It's not a man, though, is it?" I found myself asking.

"No," said my friend, sounding scared. "It isn't."

The figure 'was entirely black and like a cardboard cut-out, flat and one-dimensional. It was as if someone had taken a cookie cutter and had shaped a hole in reality in the shape of something almost, but not quite, human. And when I say black, I mean black - no light, no shade, nothing but a void. It had no features at all, and it had arms that hung down to its knees. Both Sue and I felt the creature had realised we could see it for what it really was rather than what we were supposed to see. It seemed to be ignoring us, then it seemed to realise we could see it and it began to 'lollop' faster towards us. The creature seemed to be, well, I've used the word 'lolloping' before now, which isn't really a word but denotes the dancing, jolly steps it was taking as it walked.

We ran without discussion. I got my key out and fumbled with the front door of my home, which was a big Victorian house converted into flats. Sue behind me urged me to hurry. I got the door unlocked, we dashed inside, closed, and locked it again. We ran up the stairs and hid round the corner, peeping at the front door, which had two big glass panels through which we could see the front garden. The black stick man approached the door and we could see its dark shape pressing up against the glass. Neither of us breathed. The creature looked - I say looked, it had no eyes - through first one pane, then the other. It pressed up against the glass. We couldn't breathe. It waited for what felt like an eternity before vanishing.

We didn't sleep for some time after that. To all intents and purposes, it appeared to be sauntering along the road enjoying the walk before it became shocked to see us staring at it. We instinctively felt this was not a creature to try and communicate with, this was not something that it was good to be near. We knew whatever it was, it was definitely not of the world we knew. We had not only experienced great fear but we both felt the being had been arrogant, superior in attitude and angry that its glamour had been pierced or had failed to operate. I never want to see this creature again.'

In Elkader, Iowa on February the 15th 2004 at approximately 11pm, a witness was returning to her home after finishing some work on her farm when something caught her eye as she reached her door. To her left she saw something running very fast, about 30 yards away from her. Not comprehending what she was seeing, she could only describe it as looking like "a stick man." She said that it seemed to turn its head over its left shoulder and look straight at her, then it took off in a sprint towards her front door. Very frightened, the witness ran inside quickly and locked all the doors. It took her hours to calm down. At first, she cried so hard that she started to hyperventilate. At the time, she never told anyone, not even her family, about what she had seen. She said she felt that the "thing" wanted her to see it for some reason.

Kathy Casey says: 'In May 2013, I was coming out of my studio behind my house when I saw movement. It was dark, the only lights were from my porch but they weren't enough to cast a shadow. I saw a solid shadow, no features, very tall, alongside my husband's 16 ft. tall workshop. It was very thin, about 12-13 ft tall. I could see it's outline. It had an elongated head and very long stick thin arms and fingers. It was taking large steps. I could see no facial features, but this was not a shadow; it was upright, moving fast. It felt like it was old and alien. This last thought was something I had to reject; it is just too far out of my frame of reference. At this time, I was facing it as it moved from right to left and kept going across my yard and in between our house and our neighbour's. It was taking large steps but was fast, a run even. I was so stunned. This was not a shadow thrown onto the barn, it was upright. There were no facial features that I could see. I'm not easily frightened …but now I think twice before going outside at night.'

A lady from Tennessee called the Mutual UFO Network a few years ago, not knowing who else to call and needing to urgently talk about what had just happened to her that morning. It was around 6am and she was standing on the deck of her house drinking an early morning coffee, enjoying a warm and quiet beginning to her day when suddenly she saw something that defied explanation. The deck of her house was at an elevation of twelve feet from the ground below. When she turned around to go back into the house, she stopped dead. She could not fail to see the huge black shadow in the shape of a man but standing higher than the deck. It was leaning against the deck. It was the shape of a man, yet it appeared to have no face. She was frozen to the spot, unable to move.

Suddenly it turned its 'head' toward her. Then she watched as very slowly it peeled itself off the rail of the deck. It ran its fingers slowly along the side of the rail as though it was coming in her direction. Then it started floating away.

It had legs but it wasn't touching the ground as it walked. It moved its legs like a man would, then as it got some distance away, it turned back around in her direction again. She later said that she felt very sure that it was communicating the message to her that though it had left her unharmed, it was more than capable of hurting her if it chose to do so...

One evening in October 2014, an English female healthcare administrative assistant was standing alone in her kitchen. It was almost midnight when the security light outside her house came on. Concerned that it may be a fox trying to get at the chickens she kept in the garden, she got a torch and went outside to investigate. As she approached the chicken pen, she saw a figure standing to the side. She shone the torch in his direction and saw there were two figures standing there. They appeared to be men of extremely tall height, over six foot six she estimated. She shone the light at the closest figure's face and immediately she heard a voice saying: "Please turn out the light."

"His face should have been there," she said, "but all I saw was a pointed mouth and glasses." Both of the figures were now telling her to turn off the torch and she complied. "They asked if I had seen anything 'untoward.' They were using outdated phrases," she said, "like from the 1940's, and their accents were strange." Then, as they turned to leave, she noticed they had very long feet. The same thing happened again on another occasion, only this time it was at her workplace. "I was having a cigarette at work outside and using my phone when I saw the same feet in strange shoes. I looked up and I saw this thin pale gray face staring at me. This time as I watched him walk away he made no noise and I saw that he walked like he was made out of plastic. This scared me more than anything and I felt panic. I think I'm being watched now. I constantly catch glimpses of them in passing cars, in the windows opposite my office building."

In 1968 in the town of Scarborough, Northern England, 16-year-old Adele was home alone when there was a knock at the door. Upon answering it, she was greeted by a tall man in a black suit and tie, who stood on the doorstep smiling widely at her for what she later described as an unnerving amount of time before he spoke. He asked her if she had insurance. She replied that he should come another time when her parents would be home. The man appeared to then start sweating heavily and speaking in what the girl described as "like a computerized voice."

He took off his hat and she saw that his head was bald and greatly contrasted with the colour of his face – then she realized, his face was caked in heavy make-up. He asked her if he could "See a glass of water." She took this as a request for a drink and she gestured for him to join her in the kitchen. As she handed the glass of water to him, he looked at it before placing it down on the table and did not drink it.

He noticed the clock, and asked her about it, saying, "Is that your Father's time?" Confused once more, she answered that the clock had been a gift to her Father.

The man continued, "Is it here and now?" and he began repeating the phrase over, and over again. She said it was as though he was a robot that had begun to malfunction. He kept saying the same things, and his body was jerking, then seizing-up. She said that she noticed he found it difficult to move from the spot he was standing in and did so only with some difficulty, as though his legs had locked-up.

However, she said, as he left, by the time he reached the end of the garden path and entered the street, he was walking at an ever-increasing and quite alarming speed, almost, she said, at a superhuman speed.

Frank Taylor in his work The Uninvited, describes David Ellis and his wife Caroline who were landlords of a pub in Derbyshire in the early '80's, when they were called upon at just after dawn one morning. Two men in black, wearing matching suede gloves and who "looked like twins" arrived on their doorstep that early morning.

They insisted on entering, and as they did, they removed their hats, where it was seen that they were both completely bald. What the couple most noticed however was that both men appeared to be wearing lipstick. After this visit, the husband and wife started to receive weird telephone calls. They could not decipher who was calling them, but their voice was strangely metallic.

Rev. Dr. R. W. Boeche is Pastor at Christ Lutheran Church, Lincoln, Nebraska. Author and Founder of the Fortean Research Center, he has long been involved in the study of the unexplained. He once interviewed a 29-year-old female insurance clerk 'SW' about her on-going strange encounters. She told him, "After work I was walking to the lot where I park and when I get toward my car this guy is next to my car. I figured he's trying to get into his car next to mine. But when I get closer, he doesn't look right. He was real tall and skinny, and he looked like... he was made of wax. Real pale and waxy looking.

Like maybe he was dead or something. He was looking at me all the time, and he says to me: "Do not discuss your travels. It is not safe." Real sort of precise, but in a funny flat voice, no emotion. I got to the entrance of the lot and looked back in my mirror - he was completely gone. There wasn't any way he could've got away from where I'd seen him in that little space of time!" The interviewer, Dr. R. W. Boeche asks her: "When did the 2 dead-looking guys come to your door?" "Somebody knocked at my door. There was the dead-looking guy from the parking lot, or at least somebody who looked a lot like him, and another guy who stood behind him - and looked like he could have been his brother. They both had that dead, waxy look. They said, "Your travels with the searchers. It would be unwise to discuss them with anyone." Then they kind of real jerky-like walk away, like some kind of wind-up walking doll that sort of rocks back and forth when it walks, real fast and jerky-like. I was so scared by the whole thing I broke down and cried. Spent the night in the living room with the lights on. I'm afraid they may show up again, and I don't know if I could take it. I'm afraid I'd just go crazy from it."

Karen Tooten of Postreason blog describes an incident that happened to her in the mid '70's. 'When I was 17 I was working in a small convenience store, it was somewhat isolated, when a "woman" came in to buy cigarettes. At first, I didn't pay any attention to her until I saw her hand when she handed me the money - it was not like a human hand. This startled me so I looked up and saw a very pale entity, wearing a thin black coat like a raincoat with the collar turned up to cover her neck, a heavy long-haired wig, and very large black glasses. This did not entirely hide her strange face: a very pointed chin, scant lip and nose. She did not speak. Took her cigarettes and left! Oddly, I cannot remember the details of her hand though it was the first thing I noticed. Nor do I think she left in a car which was odd since most patrons drove up to the store - it was isolated. I wasn't paying much attention to her until I saw her hand. She was startlingly strange-looking. Other details that really jumped out at me like her hand, her facial features were not human-looking. Whatever she was, the memory of her face has stuck with me to this day. But what I find really odd is that her hand - I cannot remember, the visual is completely gone. As to the gender of the cigarette "lady" I have never been certain of that.'

A research friend of mine, who detailed his life-long series of strange encounters in our book 'The Story of the Harlequin,' says, 'I had just graduated high school in 1994. The weekend that followed graduation was a cornucopia of graduation parties and other gatherings. On that night in 1994 I left a graduation party with some of my friends. I had to drive a couple of them to the other side of town where they lived. It was late and only a few cars were out. We were headed north on 76th street and were stopped at the traffic light on 76th and Oklahoma Avenue on the southwest of Milwaukee. When the light turned green, we noticed what appeared to be a young woman with blonde hair on the east side of the street. She had come out from behind a video store on the corner. As she walked, we noticed that her movements were very jerky. In those days there was a small park on the northwest corner of that intersection where a few junkies used to loiter. My initial thought was she was possibly a part of that group. However, one of the guys in my car thought he knew who this young girl was. As we got closer, I began to slow down. She seemed to notice us at that moment. With every step she took, her movements became more exaggerated. As she walked her hair bounced more violently. Something was very wrong with what I was seeing. We were now crossing paths as she began to walk toward my car. From only a few feet away I saw her clear as the day through the passenger side window. It was wearing a wig and pretending to be a "normal" person walking down the street. From the back seat someone said, "Oh my God her eyes!" A panic struck everyone. I was told to floor it, which I did without hesitation. We flew down 76th street doing at least 60 miles per hour until we were far enough away to feel somewhat safe. No matter how far away we were, each person struggled to get out of the car out of fear that this strange woman might be waiting for them in some dark shadow. Even though most of us were now legally adults, we were still not mature enough to grasp who or what we had just seen. There was no frame of reference. Someone said they believed that she was a dead person. Of all the possibilities discussed in panic that night, it was by far the most apt. Her face certainly did not have the same life in it that your face or my face have.

As terrible of an experience as that night was, the situation would become much worse for everyone. One of my friends from that night died of cancer only a few years later. The others became involved with bad crowds, ended up becoming addicts or doing time in prison. That night seemed to be a harbinger of bad luck for all of us. I am still plagued by the thought of what would have happened if I was on foot that night. What if I had run into her alone on that empty street? It seems so obvious to me that there would have been no trace left of me. I would have seen her eyes and died in my fear. Yet it was not only my terror. Others had now seen her as well and felt her power. To this very day, I cannot even say for certain if it is male or female. It seems beyond all such designations.'

In 2012, The Glasgow South and Eastwood Extra uncovered a rarely known Scottish tale called 'The Gurning Man.' It was a phenomenon which occurred in the Crosshill district of Glasgow, in the 1970's. Accounts began to circulate about a strange and disturbing figure who was appearing at night. Some of the words used to describe this figure were that he looked "demented" and "unnatural." He appeared in human form, but his appearance was so disturbing that a number of female residents went so far as to move away from the area, to ensure they would never encounter him again; so great was the fear he engendered. An unnamed woman in her fifties, who lived with her husband and children, was awoken one night by a strange snorting sound. Upon opening her eyes, she saw a figure standing at the foot of the bed. It looked like a man, but as she looked at his face, lit-up through the gap in the curtains from the streetlamp outside, she saw his grin, and it was unnaturally wide. He was grinning at her "maniacally" while simultaneously rubbing his hands fast up and down his chest. She let out a blood-curdling scream which woke her husband, who on instinct jumped from the bed to turn on the bedroom light. As the light came on, the bedroom appeared to be empty. A few days prior to this, unbeknown to this couple, two teenage girls had reported their own horrifying encounter. The girls had been walking home late one night within walking distance of this couple's house when it happened. There was an almost full moon that night and so, although it was dark, they could see the road quite clearly as they walked. Suddenly, a man appeared in front of them, coming toward them. His appearance was decidedly strange. The girls estimated that he looked quite old, he was bald, and he was almost skeletal. He was dressed all in black. As he walked, his movements were oddly jittery, almost as though he was excessively agitated, or a robot. As he drew nearer, the girls began to feel the hairs on the back of their necks stand up, and they fell into a terrified silence as he got closer. They picked up their walking pace, hoping to pass him by as quickly as possible, and after passing him with their heads down, they turned around to look back at him. His face had the strangest expression. They described it as "contorted" and "grimacing" and his grin was "unnaturally wide." This alarming grin was accompanied by the most awful sounds of grunting and snorting. The girls began to run, glancing round one last time to see that, to their surprise, he no longer stood there. There was no way he could have disappeared from sight so fast. There was nowhere for him to go. The long wide road was now empty, but there was no-where for him to have hidden. No houses, no trees. There were more reports in the same district too. One morning, an elderly resident saw him standing in the middle of the road, looking "agitated and jittery." Then he vanished in front of her eyes. In another case, the police were called to the occupiers of one home who believed there was a burglar in the house. The same figure, dressed all in black and with an impossibly large grin, disappeared in front of their eyes. There were more than fifteen separate encounters in all, and all from witnesses who had no knowledge of the other reported incidents. Then the reports stopped. The riddle of who, or what this grinning, gurning man was, was never solved.

In this last strange encounter, my researcher friend Dan say, 'One morning on my way to work I stopped at a gas station around 5am. I was standing in an aisle when this short, stocky man came into the station. He walked with an awkward gait. He looked as if he were dragging himself through the aisles. My first thought was that he was hurt, or maybe that he had been in a car accident. Every step he took seemed to hurt him. The man didn't appear to be looking at anything on the shelves, he was just walking up and down the aisles aimlessly. I remember feeling fear at the sight of him. The woman behind the counter didn't seem to notice the man, which I felt was quite strange. Days before seeing this man at the gas station I was looking through some old pictures. I came across one from the early 1980's where I had been standing near a bonfire with my family at our cottage near Eagle River, Wisconsin. In the photo I was wearing a baseball cap with the logo of a now defunct dog food company. For some reason the design on the baseball cap was stuck in my mind the following morning before I had arrived at the gas station. Now as the man dragged himself through the aisles, there was this overwhelming smell of rotten meat lingering in the air. Even the clerk seemed to notice it. As I got a closer look at the man, he appeared bloated and discolored. He was wearing a pair of beat up jeans and a faded t-shirt with a flannel shirt over it. He just didn't look right. On his head was the exact same baseball cap I had been wearing in the picture of me at the bonfire with my family. I had just looked at that picture a few hours earlier. I didn't know what to think. It was too much of a coincidence. The man looked like Frankenstein's monster. He seemed to be cobbled together with mismatched body parts, which is why it seemed like he was dragging himself in excruciating pain like a zombie when he walked. As I meandered through the aisles that morning, I caught a brief glimpse of his eyes, which to me appeared as though they were painted on his closed eyelids. There was just no way the eyes were real. I did not want to look at him for very long because I knew that to do so would be dangerous. The man appeared to be dead. He was an animated and bloated corpse walking around a 7/11, which sounds absolutely preposterous to sane and rational people. He never said a word to me or anyone else. He circled around the station and just walked out. There were no overt threatening gestures made toward me or the clerk. I understood that seeing him that morning was a message being made directly to me. The baseball cap on his head was giving me a subtle message, "This will be you if you continue to act out of line".

Who or what are these "people," and what do they want with us?

Chapter Twenty-Six:

The Vampyres

Hidden away among ancient tall trees in the Boldu-Creteasca forest of Romania, there is a small pond with a sinister reputation. It is not a deep pond and it is a pond that few would even know was there unless they walked right up to it. The pond is filled with dark algae and is not attractive or appealing. It would be best not to go there actually; it would be best to avoid this pond, for it has a dark history and a bad reputation. It is called 'The Witches Pond.' It is a cursed place, it is said.

Locals do not go to this pond, because they know of its history. Romania Journal explains; 'They say the patch of water is surrounded by forces from other worlds and unexplainable events occur in this place.' Lightning can appear suddenly and violently above this pool with thrashing rain and storms. You will not see wildlife here, and the local people say animals and birds refuse to drink the water. It was once a place where witches would gather on important dates in their calendar, like Saint Gheorghe's night, and they would carry out strange rituals here. 'It seems that every spell or curse said on the pond's shore came true,' says the Journal. There are reports of dark-robed figures still meeting at this pond.

It is also famously known as the location where Vlad Tepes, the real Dracula of the 15th century, was betrayed by his warriors when they turned on him, seized him and decapitated him here at the site of this small pond tucked away in the forest. They threw his body into the pond, and it is said that his blood made the water turn red. Dracula's body was dragged from the pond by monks at the nearby monastery, and they buried him in their grounds, but ever since then, strange things have happened here, including unexplained murders. In 1977, a terrible earthquake devastated the region and many people were killed. It is said that the country's Dictator, Nicolae Ceausescu instructed some of the bodies be thrown into the pond, rather than be properly and respectfully buried. The pond was duly filled to the brim with corpses. Local people say that within days, all of the corpses had vanished. To this day, no-one can account for how that happened.

In more recent times, a story is told about the pond which involves a young woman and a violent man. The story goes that the young woman was dragged into the forest by this man and as they reached the cursed pond, he attempted to assault her. As she struggled with him, he hit her and it knocked her unconscious. When she woke up, he was no longer attacking her. As she glanced around nervously, expecting to see him, all she could see were ripped and bloody body parts of the man who had attacked her, scattered all around her. The local police later said it was impossible that she could have done this to the man herself. The man, they said, looked like he had been attacked by wild bear; but there are no large animals like that in this forest.

Had it been a vampire, in the very spot where the original vampire, Vlad Tepes, had been decapitated? Says one Romanian man, 'Their true name comes from the Romanian term 'strig' or 'strigat,' which means 'scream,' because before they attack, you can hear a very terrifying scream like no animal or human can make. They can be children or adults who were very violent while they were alive, and in some cases, there are signs even from birth of a man or woman who can become a strigoi after death. When they are very well fed, they can appear almost normal at night.' He says they act by 'trying to lure people into the forest or dark places if they are in a city, so it can kill without being disturbed. A starving strigoi will almost decapitate the victim when it is feeding, leaving the crime scene looking like an animal attack.' He says he has never been to the forest, but, 'I know about some who died there. I was 16 years old when it happened. An older boy from my neighbourhood and some of his friends went to some relatives near Boldu-Creteasca forest.' 'When they returned, while passing by the forest, they had a car accident. There were three boys and two girls. Two boys and one girl died in the accident including the boy I knew, but the other two were not found in the car or near the car. They ran into the forest and were found in front of the pond, both dead; the girl with an open mouth like she was screaming when she died and the boy was found

without a hand. The hand was never found as far as I know. And both of them had their chests crushed.'
'A couple of years ago, I also heard in the news about some teenagers who were camping there. They disappeared. Nothing was found except for a couple of drops of blood in one of their tents.'

Chapter Twenty-Seven:

The Children who disappeared into the Mountain

The English Poet Robert Browning immortalized the story of the Pied Piper in the 1800's with his poem 'The Pied Piper of Browning.' It's a story that was told to children from generation to generation, and it gained a permanent place alongside The Brothers Grimm fairytales of Snow White and Sleeping Beauty. This tale of the Pied Piper however, while as rich and fantastical in folkloric detail as these fairytales, is actually based on a true event. It took place in the small rural town of Brunswick, in the county of Hamelin, near Hanover in Germany. The year was 1284 A.D. and the event was recorded in the official town records, and later memorialized in a stained-glass window of the Church there. This window which displayed the record of the missing children, was destroyed along with the Church in a blaze in 1660. However, a number of written accounts held in other places have survived. The mountain where the children disappeared is called

Poppenberg, and it is a tree-covered mountain within the Harz National Park. Inside the Park there are hidden villages with quaint timber framed homes, old castles, and closed-down mines. It's also a nature reserve with a landscape of forest, moors, and rivers.

The story of the Pied Piper goes that in the village, a plague of rats descended. They ate their way through all the stores of food, attacked and bit people while they slept, and generally terrified everyone with their wild rampaging. As the villagers faced a rapidly diminishing food supply, and with the town's officials running out of ideas on how to try to drive the rats out of town, an emergency meeting was held at the town hall. The villagers were furious and they were scared and they demanded an urgent resolution to the catastrophe. The town counsellors retreated to a private room to debate what to do when suddenly there was a knock at the door. The Mayor instructed the person on the other side of the door to enter, and as the poem describes, in came a rather mysterious person.

'In did come the strangest figure! A wandering fellow with a gipsy coat of red and yellow. And he himself was tall and thin. Lips where smiles went out and in. There was no guessing his kith and kin! Quoth one: "It's as if my great-grandsire, Starting up at the Trump of Doom's tone, Had walked this way from his painted tomb!" The figure standing in the doorway looks like a walking cadaver, brightly-dressed yet looking like the living dead. He tells the Mayor that for a price, he is able to solve their problem. "I'm able, by means of a secret charm, to draw all creatures beneath the sun after me. People call me the Pied Piper."

The councillors find themselves intrigued by this odd-looking man, and almost hypnotized by him. They were also desperate. However, they all agreed that the price he was asking was much too high; yet they were at their wits' end, and so finally the Mayor agreed he would pay the Piper if he could drive out the hordes of rats from the village. So, the strange-looking fellow got to work. 'Into the street the Piper stept, smiling first a little smile, as if he knew what magic slept in his quiet pipe. From street to street he piped advancing, and step for step they followed dancing.'

As if by some miracle, all the rats followed faithfully behind him. With his magickal pipe, the rats ran behind him as he played his curious tune, and as he reached the River Weser, they threw themselves into the water and drowned. The villagers were so relieved that the rats were gone. However, the Piper had named his price for the job and now the Mayor decided not to pay. Over the years, this tale has been interpreted as an allegory about greedy corporate types who cheat their poorer fellow man, and yet, very strangely, the majority of the older historical accounts and records of the incident do not mention a plague of rats at all; but they do all mention the missing children.

In the story, the Mayor offers the Pied Piper only a trifle of the sum agreed. The strangely dressed cadaver-like figure is not happy with this. He tells the Mayor threateningly, "Folks who put me in a passion may find me pipe to another fashion." It is a very dangerous threat, and yet the Mayor does not understand what the Piper means by it, until he demonstrates. The Piper begins to play his pipe once more, but this time, it is not the rats who follow him as he plays his mystical tune; it's all the village children, who are following blindly behind him just like the rats did, as though hypnotized by his music, as though they have no power to resist him. The children follow him unfalteringly, all of them following him in unison, forming a long procession behind his bright coat-tails as he leads them out of the village and into the forest. The Mayor and his officials, and all of the children's parents seem unable to physically move to run after them and try to stop them. It is as if they have all been frozen on the spot. As the children reach the mountainside, "A wondrous portal opened wide, as if a cavern was suddenly hollowed." In went the Piper, and all of the children, never to be seen again.

This is the poetic version; however, many written historical accounts also appear to back up this story; aside from the plague of rats itself, which is curious indeed. Who was this odd and disturbing character who arrived to lead the children away? The first historical account in the stained-glass window of the village Church does not speak of rats or of the Piper. After this, probably the earliest known written record is that found in the Decan Lude of Hamelin's Chorus Book, written in the late 1380's, in which there is an account in Latin by an eye-witness to the event. However, we do not meet the Pied Piper until the Lueneburg Manuscript from the 1440's. 'In 1284 on June 26, by a piper clothed in many colors, 130 children were seduced and lost near the hillside.' In 1556, we have J. Fincelius' De Miraculis sui Temporis, translated as 'The Miracles of Time,' which also describes the story, and determines that the Piper is the Devil. It is not until the Chronicles of Zimmern, by the Count F. Von Zimmern, around 1560, that rats are mentioned in the tale. Does this suggest that the real reason for the disappearance of all of the village children had nothing at all to do with a rat infestation? The first time the tale is written in the English language is in 1605 in Restitution of Decayed Intelligence, by Richard Verstegan. He suggests that the children re-appeared in Transylvania.

There are no doubts in any of the records that the children did indeed disappear en-masse in a real event, but what happened to them? There are varying views about this. One theory is that the children were victim to the Black Plague. However, surely the plague would have killed old and young, not just the children? And, the most prevalent time of the Black Plague in Europe was between 1347 – 1351, and this was almost a century after the children disappeared. Another theory is that the children could have been taken to fight as child soldiers in The Crusades. Indeed, the term 'Children' could have been a euphemism for the young men of the village going off to fight, perhaps recruited to fight without any real choice in the matter, and then they were killed on the battlefield.

The Children's' Crusade, in which thousands of children marched to the Holy Land, with many dying on the way or being sold into servitude, happened in 1212 however, more than 30 years before the Pied Piper arrived in

Hamelin. And, while there was also fighting in Europe over various territories too, this was not taking place in Germany in 1284 A.D., and so why would young men from that particular rural village have been taken to fight as child soldiers?

Some advanced researchers including linguist Jurgen Udolph, suggest the theory that the young men of the village were émigrés. 'Bishops and dukes of Pomerania and Brandenburg sent out glib "lokators," or 'recruitment officers,' who would offer riches for those who were willing to move to new lands. Some of them were brightly dressed, and all were silver-tongued.' The linguist believed that the children were re-located to Poland, after finding similar surnames in the populace there. But wouldn't their parents have gone too?

In 1650, Jesuit monk Athanasius Kirchner spoke of having seen a Transylvanian journal in which there were descriptions of 'kidnapped' folk from the village, living in a Saxon colony in Transylvania, not Poland. Indeed, Robert Browning's poem states, 'In Transylvania there's a tribe of alien people who ascribe the outlandish ways and dress (of) their neighbours, to their fathers and mothers having risen out of some subterraneous prison into which they were trepanned a long time ago out of Hamelin.' 'Trepanned' meaning kidnapped. Curiously however, he adds, 'But how or why, they don't understand,' again, indicating the mystery enshrouding the event. He is saying that they have no recollection of how they got there. Then there is researcher Wolfgang Mieder who said he found historical documents to show that the people from the

Village had settled in Romania. Other researchers say that just because similar surnames were found in other countries, it does not make for corroboration or proof they went to any of these countries; and, if the villagers all relocated, not just the children, wouldn't the historical records in 1264 have mentioned this? All records say only the children disappeared from the village, not their parents. Many documentarians in earlier centuries interpreted the tale of the Piper as being without doubt the Devil, who had transported the children to Hell itself. In Robert Burton's 1621 The Anatomy of Melancholy, like some before him, he writes, 'In likeness of a Piper, the Devil carried away the children that were never seen after. On St. Mary Magdalene's Day, the Devil went about the streets visibly in human form, piped and allured many children, boys and girls, and led them through the town gate towards a mountain. There he disappeared with the numerous children.' Hiob Fincelus in 1556 also give his account of the Devil arriving in Hamelin, while others thought the Piper was a Demon. The villagers were less literate than in contemporary times and so the keeping of journals and diaries would have been less prevalent, so it is difficult to find first-hand accounts of the event. It is curious that no official town records exist explaining the cause of the vanishing of all the children.

The story has been passed down through generations across Europe as a fairy tale, with most people not realizing it is a true story, and yet the fate of the children remains unknown. The most intriguing theory is that the children vanished into another world, or another dimension. Perhaps this is the case, no matter how fantastical this sounds, for when the Mayor of the village refuses to pay the money he agreed, the gaudily-dressed Piper replies, "I can't wait, I've promised to visit Baghdad by dinner-time.' Is this simply literary license and fantasy in the poem, or did Browning wish to infer that the 'strange fellow' was in fact a man possessed of supernatural abilities, and able to re-appear in the City of Baghdad in another country thousands of miles away? How could he do this other than by supernatural means? Or by time-travel or teleportation? 'As they reached the mountain-side, A wondrous portal opened wide.'

Some huge cavern suddenly appeared in the hillside and swallowed up the children, who some say, then re-appeared in some far-off country, though town records make no mention of them ever re-appearing again. The translation of the words in the historical town records state that the Piper took the children to 'the place of execution,' which have led some historians to state that the children were ritually sacrificed to the Devil. However, the term 'Place of Execution,' more rationally could be explained as 'the spot' or 'the place' in which the event or action took place; that being their abduction, rather than that they were literally killed by execution.

The instrument which the Pied Piper played is one of the world's first musical instruments and it became known as the Flute. The ancient Etruscan's would use their flutes to lure wild boars into traps. Ovid wrote in 'Metamorphoses,' of Pan, the horned God of the forests, who sat beside the river fashioning reeds from the riverbank to make a musical instrument. Pan is depicted with the upper body of a human but the lower body of a goat and a goat's head with horns on its head. Being the guardian of the forest, his reputation was that he would cause terror in the woods to unsuspecting travellers who ventured into his domain. Some biblical scholars say this goat-man was produced by the Fallen Angels who procreated with women and produced hideous contorted creatures with supernatural powers. Could the Pied Piper have been one of these? And yet, in appearance, he looked more like a ghost, or zombie. It was as though he had risen up from the grave and come back to life. Who was this extraordinary fellow? And where did he take the children?

Chapter Twenty-Eight:

The Hexham Heads

It's a tale of strange twin stone heads discovered buried in a garden, a half-man half-beast appearing in bedrooms, and archaeologists appearing to become distressed or possessed: this is the story of 'The Hexham Heads.'

Hexham is the name of a small northern market town. It is 20 miles west of the English city of Newcastle upon Tyne, and located a few miles from Hadrian's Wall, a defensive fortification built by the Romans in 122 AD. One February afternoon in 1972, 11-year-old Colin Robson was playing in his garden at the family home of 3 Rede Avenue, Hexham. He was having a go at weeding when he looked down at a lump in the ground that appeared to be a large stone approximately the size of a tennis ball. As he looked closer, he saw that there appeared to be a conical protrusion on one side of the object. Clearing away the grass and earth around it, he reached down to pick it up, and he saw that it appeared to have human features on it, like a face. The young boy was filled with excitement at his unusual find and he shouted for his brother Leslie to come and see what he had discovered. Leslie was astonished at his brother's discovery and not to be outdone, he frantically started to dig the ground. It was not long before Leslie too had found a second strange head.

One of the heads appeared to be a 'boy' and the other a 'girl.' They were a pale, greenish stone colour. The boy had short hair carved into his head. Both of their faces were carved too. Neither of the stone faces were pretty – but the girl's was the worst. She would go on to be given the name 'the Hag,' for she had a large hook nose and what was described as 'Wild bulging eyes.' It seemed that the protrusions that stuck out at an angle, were their necks.

Dr Kenneth Bryophy of Glasgow University, calls the find, 'One of the most remarkable and controversial examples of urban prehistory that I can think of. These frankly weird objects were found in a normal garden and consisting of a pair of fist-sized stone heads with creepy little faces.' The discovery of the two strange heads was to see the start of a chain of events that 'quickly escalated until museums, archaeologists, geologists, the media - all wanted a piece of the action. What makes this an especially weird story, is that it draws on another type of archaeology - sinister stones, ancient rites and dealing with things we cannot comprehend.' It's a strange story, full of inexplicable and disturbing events and a cast of characters. After Colin and Leslie's discovery of the heads, they rushed indoors with them to show their parents, and this would initiate the odd chain of events. It all began when the family came downstairs the next morning to find that the heads had moved position. They now seemed to be facing an entirely different direction from the one they had been left in on the mantelpiece when the family had gone to bed. The heads had seemingly rotated during the night while the family were asleep. The boys denied any part in moving them, as did the rest of the family!

There were other strange incidents too. One night, one of the daughter's beds was showered with glass, and the two daughters who shared that bedroom were quick to move out of it. According to Paul Screeton, a northern journalist who investigated the case in the 1970's for his book 'Quest for the Hexham Heads,' the family said a strange flower sprang up in the garden where one of the heads had been dug up. It would somehow glow iridescently in the night. Also, 'After the burial of their budgerigar, one night they saw a mysterious bright light a short distance above the ground, where they had buried the bird.' But it was not just their house that was affected. Mrs. Eileen Dodds and her family who lived in the house next door, were too. Mrs. Dodds had been sleeping in one of her children's bedrooms, as her child had been unwell. She suddenly woke startled to find a half-beast, half-man creature standing in her bedroom. When it saw that she was awake and staring at it, she said it turned and "padded" downstairs and went out of the front door!

She told a Tyneside Newspaper in 1972, "I had gone into the children's bedroom to sleep with one of them who was unwell and my ten-year-old son Brian, kept telling me that he felt something touching him. I told him not to be so silly. Then I saw this shape. It came towards me and I definitely felt it touch me on the legs. Then, on all fours, it moved out of the room. I was absolutely terrified and screamed out for my husband."

Next door, Colin and Leslie's mother Mrs. Robson later said that on the same night, she heard a cracking sound and screams coming from next door. Mrs. Dodds told Mrs. Robson that those sounds came from a thing that looked like a Werewolf. Now, it has to be said that one researcher back then, Stuart Ferrol for the Fortean Times Magazine said that he heard of a local prank that happened the same night, which involved a drunk man and a stolen sheep carcass on his back, that had been stolen from a nearby abattoir, and that he'd been seen staggering up Rede Road where they all lived. Did this prank really happen? And if it did, it would be a remarkable coincidence that Mrs. Dodds would seem to see a half-man half-sheep in her bedroom! Although how and quite why the man would have got into her bedroom, at the risk of arrest and jail, was not explained. For Mrs. Dodds however, this was no mere mortal man. She became so terrified afterwards that she went to her local council and asked them to re-house her somewhere else. The council were surprisingly sympathetic, and they actually agreed to move her to another house, after hearing her describe her terrible night-time ordeal.

Scientist Dr. Don Robbins, a chemist who became involved in the investigation into the mysterious origins of the heads, on hearing of this strange night-time visitor, drew a tentative parallel between the half-man half sheep seen in Mrs. Dodds bedroom and a creature from Norse mythology called 'The Wulver;' a powerful and dangerous creature, he said.

Next to come into the story was a lorry driver called Des Craigie. He had been a life-long resident of Hexham, and when the discovery of the stone heads began to be reported in the local and national Newspapers, and archaeologist and scientists began to form theories about the origin of these ancient heads, he came forward to the local paper to claim that he had actually created the two heads himself, from concrete, and that he had once lived in the house where the heads had been discovered, at 3 Rede Avenue. He told the Newcastle Chronicle that he had made the heads to entertain his daughter when she was a child.

Rather embarrassingly, this revelation came after many leading figures in the disciplines of archaeology and science had been studying the heads thinking them to be ancient artefacts, and indeed, one leading archaeologist had declared them to be ancient Celtic Heads. This archaeologist, Dr. Anne Ross, said that after much investigation, she had come to the conclusion that these heads were of Romano-Celtic origin and part of the Pagan 'Head-cult' tradition. The Celts had settled in North East England and they were known to revere the human head as a gruesome totem. The practise of the Celts was such that they would set the severed heads of their vanquished enemies over the doors of their houses and barns. This practise had been particularly rife in West Yorkshire and Northumberland, where Hexham was. Dr. Ross believed that the stone heads found by the boys would have been part of a Celtic shrine. These newly-discovered heads were symbolic of 'otherworldly powers' she said, although the Professor admitted that she was struggling to pin down the date that these heads had been created. She went on to write about her findings in Journal Arhcaeologia Aelina, in 1973.

Meanwhile, Professor Frank Hodson of the University of Southampton said in his opinion, the heads were comprised of sandstone, while Dr Douglas Robson of Newcastle University determined that 'the material from which the heads have been formed is an artificial cement,' which would seem to imply that, in his opinion, these heads were not thousands of years old, as Dr Anne Ross believed. Meanwhile,

Dr Robbins, the chemist and the originator of the claim that the bedroom appearance of a half-man half-beast in Mrs Dodd's bedroom was most likely 'The Wulver,' collaborated on a book called 'The Secret Language of Stone' with Dr Anne Ross; she of the 'Celtic head cult' claim. Robbins determined, that in his opinion the material from which the heads had been formed was 'unlike any natural sandstone,' and he became convinced that the heads added proof to the theory of 'Stone-Tape.' This was a theory first developed in the 19th-century by psychic researchers such as Charles Babbage, and it is the idea that natural objects become saturated with memories of events that have happened and the emotions evoked during these events, and that stone can 'record' and 're-play' these memories like ghosts, and that this can cause hauntings and even poltergeists. The two stone heads, Robson the chemist proposed, were behaving like tape-recorders and replaying past events; hence the appearance of the Were-creature, The Wulver, which he believed had really once existed.

Lorry driver Des Craigie meanwhile was adamant that he had created the heads himself in the 1950's. When he discovered his son reading about the heads in a new Reader's Digest book 'Folklore Myths and Legends,' featuring Dr. Anne Ross' proclamation that these heads were very ancient Celtic cult heads, he contacted the editor of the publication to ask him to remove the false story, although it did not end up being removed, presumably because the book was already out in print.

The lorry driver was insistent; "Nancy played with them as dolls!" These were modern creations, he said, and he'd actually made three of them. "One got broken and I threw it in the bin. The others just got kicked around and must have landed up where the lads found them. To say that they were old would be conning people."

Mr. Craigie managed to be reunited with the heads briefly, after they'd been given to the Newcastle Museum of Antiquities. Two resident archaeology experts, Roger Miket and David Smith determined that these stone heads were very likely thousands of years old. According to Peter Brookesmith, editor of Phenomenon Magazine, the lorry driver astounded the curator at the Museum with his claims, and when he asked to see them, the curator, believing of course that these were precious historic relics, became alarmed. She was 'so security conscious that she would not allow them to be viewed until another officer was present,' for the curator obviously believed they were highly rare artefacts and feared damage might be done to them without proper and careful handling. The lorry driver reiterated to her; they weren't rare, they were a mere 16 years old! The British Museum in London also had possession of the heads for a time – but the museum gave them back. It was said that the staff there had become unsettled by strange happenings and it was decided that the heads should no longer be kept there, for the sake of their staff.

Meanwhile, the lorry driver offered to make some new heads; to prove that the two heads dug up by the boys were actually his heads. However, rather oddly, the new heads he made did not particularly seem to bear any real resemblance to the newly dug-up heads! Which then caused those who were sceptical of his claims to cast doubt on the veracity of his story. This doubt particularly gave fuel to Dr. Anne Ross, who chimed in with; "Mr Craigie's claim is an interesting story. Unless Mr. Craigie was familiar with genuine Celtic stone heads it would be extraordinary for him to make them like this. They are not crude by any means." She continued to insist they were at least 800 years old. Curiously though, the lorry driver was not the only one in Hexham claiming to have made or be making heads! Almost as though this was an omen of things to come, 'Another bizarre aspect of the tale,' Screeton says, 'Two months before the brothers rediscover the originals in Rede Avenue, Colin Robson, then 11, made a clay model head at junior school, similar to those which were discovered in Rede Avenue. "It was for a competition," Colin told me. "I'd never made anything like it before. The master said it was ugly and commented that it should have had a proper neck."'' How strange! 'For completeness,' Screeton says, 'I should add that the repulsive-looking head, painted black, brown, red and blue, and with two broken fangs, was judged second in the contest!' Mrs Robson, the boy's mother told the Press: "It is remarkable in its likeness to the heads found in the garden. Colin said the idea of making this head just came to him!"' However, no-one felt it was possible that Colin or his brother had made the two heads they had dug up, and Screeton adds that Dr. Anne Ross continued to, 'Refer to the folklore of the heads within this context of "a belief in its powers of averting evil and keeping the supernatural at bay", yet for most, it is far from apposite in reference to the scarifying manifestations.' In other words, Screeton meant, if they were ancient totems of protection, they weren't not doing a very good job! Instead of keeping evil out, they seemed to be letting evil in! In fact, not only were museums handing them back, but Dr. Ross herself would be next to find herself victim to some disturbing encounters, after she took possession of the heads. Dr. Ross, who one would imagine to be a rational scientist, would soon find her house had become host to 'The Wulver' too, after she took the heads home. Dr. Ross said she woke one night around 2 a.m. feeling very cold and very fearful, and saw the most astonishing sight. "I woke up and felt extremely frightened. In fact, panic-stricken, and terribly, terribly cold. There was a sort of dreadful atmosphere of icy coldness all round me and something made me look towards the door, and as I looked, I saw this... thing going out of it. It was about 6 feet high, slightly stooping, and it was black against the white door.

It was half animal and half man. The upper part I would have said was a wolf and the lower part was human, and I would have said that it was covered with a kind of black, very dark fur. It went out and I just saw it clearly and then it disappeared and something made me run after it; a thing I wouldn't normally have done, but I felt compelled to run after it. I got out of bed and I ran and I could hear it going down the stairs, then it disappeared towards the back of the house."

Dr. David Clark, Deputy Vice-Chancellor of Bristol University and teacher of Law, but also a life-long researcher of the unexplained said, 'When I interviewed Ross in 1994, she told me the stones brought an "Evil presence" with them. "There was no doubt the haunting was that of a werewolf," she told me. "The thing took form very gradually, and when it actually became not just audible and hinted at, but tangible and visible, something had to be done, because it was definitely growing…" The house was subsequently exorcised, Dr Clark says.

On another occasion, Dr. Ross came home with her husband Richard, also an archaeologist, to find their daughter Bernice very distressed. When they asked her what was wrong, she managed to explain that she had come home earlier that afternoon to find a large black shape rushing down the stairs. As it reached half-way down the staircase, it apparently vaulted over the bannister, landing on the floor with a soft thud on padded animal-feet. Dr Ross and her husband rushed through the house to see if there was perhaps an intruder; but none could be found in any of the rooms – and the description of the creature sounded very much like the half-man half-beast Ross had seen in her bedroom. Interestingly, at the turn of the 20th Century in the same area, a Wolf was said to be roaming loose, and this was just a few minutes from the location where the two heads had been found. It was known as 'The Wolf of Allendale.'

"Wolf at large in Allendale" said the headlines of the Hexham Currant on December the 10th, 1904. In the three preceding weeks, farmers around the village of Allendale had been waking to find many of their livestock had inexplicably vanished or were found terribly mutilated, with hideous wounds. Many had been disembowelled or decapitated, with their heads missing or missing bodies. The finger of suspicion was pointed immediately at a Captain Bain of nearby Shotley Bridge, who owned a large grey wolf. However, after the local constabulary looked into it, they discovered that this wolf was only an infant of just over 4 months old, and they said it was far too small to be capable of marauding and massacring entire herds of sheep at night. The locals began to fear that the beast responsible had to be a creature of mythical proportions, or of supernatural origins, and it was stalking the vicinity; for what else was capable of such destruction, they nervously wondered, and what else was it capable of? Hysteria soon set in, for Wolves had long- since been extinct in this area. There were no wild wolves here. Women and children were warned that they must stay indoors after sundown. Big lamps were lit, to burn all night in an attempt to scare off the wolf. The local Member of Parliament, Major Wentworth Henry Canning Beaumont put forward a reward of £5 for the Wolf's skin; a considerable sum in those days, and the 'The Hexham Wolf Committee' was set up. Soon, a posse of over 100 men all formed together, armed with lanterns and shotguns, and a systematic hunt for the wolf began. They even brought in a renowned pack of hunting dogs called 'The Haydon Hounds,' who were known for their excellent ability to track down wild animals. However, this expert pack of dogs could not find the wolf, nor could they even find any scent to track. Through winter, the hunt continued; but to no avail. Sheep were still disappearing, or being discovered horribly mutilated, or almost entirely eaten. The invisible attacker struck night after night. The Hexham Wolf Committee were at a loss about what to do: until they came up with the idea of summoning a famed hound who went by the name of 'Monarch.' The famous fortean Charles Fort wrote in the early 1900's, that when 'The celebrated bloodhound arrived, it was with such a look of sagacity that the sheep farmers troubles were supposed to be over. The wise dog was put on what was supposed to be the trail of the wolf. But, if there weren't any wolf, who can blame a celebrated bloodhound for not smelling something that wasn't? The dog sniffed. Then he sat down. It was impossible to set this dog on the trail of a wolf, though each morning he was taken to a place of fresh slaughter.' The invisible wolf was yet again impossible to track, impossible to find.

Next, The Wolf Committee turned to their last option; 'In came a Mr. Biddick to save the day.' Like the famous hound, Monarch, Mr. Biddick was a renowned tracker too, and he surely could not fail, for his reputation preceded him. The Hexham Herald declared, "The right man, at last!" and Fort describes Biddick's arrival, which was greeted with much expectation and desperation. 'The Wolf Committee met him at the station. There was a plaid shawl strapped to his back, and the flaps of his hunting cap were considered unprecedented. Almost everybody had confidence in the shawl, or felt that the flaps were authoritative. The devices by which he covered his ears made beholders feel that they were in the presence of Science.' Mr Biddick was a big game hunter. Yet, much as he tried, he too failed to pick up on the trail of the beast. There were no tracks to follow and no scent could be found. The sheep slaughter continued apace. 'Four sheep were killed at Low Eschelles, and one at Sedham, in one night. On both sides of the River Tyne, something kept on slaughtering.'

Meanwhile, the tracker Mr Biddick was 'going from farm to farm, sifting and dating and classifying observations: drawing maps, card-indexing his data,' but still no luck. Then, on December 29th, the local Courier announced, 'Wolf killed on a railroad line!' This was at Cumwinton, a hamlet 30 miles away from Hexham. However, all the experts said this wolf was not capable of killing the sheep. It was not big enough, not strong enough, they said. By the end of January however, all sheep attacks had stopped. Not much is known about the wolf found at Cumwinton, as it seems the locals were just so relieved that the seemingly preternatural attacks had ceased, and so all we know is that the experts involved proclaimed that it wasn't this wolf who had killed all the sheep, but yet the attacks did indeed end. Quite how this wolf would have travelled without leaving any tracks or any scent to follow, no longer mattered; for the attacks had stopped and the mystery left to fade into the distance, as the farmers livelihood was no longer at stake and the women and children were just glad to be allowed outside again.

Back then to the continuing story of the Hexham Heads, and Dr. Anne Ross was insisting: the Wolf-creature that had appeared in her bedroom and that frightened her daughter home-alone, was very real. Or rather, they had really seen it. "It was not something shadowy or only glimpsed out the corner of the eye." It was solid and it was noisy, and, "Everyone who came to the house commented on a definite presence of evil," she told Dr. David Clark, and she insisted it appeared on more than one occasion. Dr. Ross was so unnerved that she not only gave away the two Hexham Heads so that they were no longer in her house, but she gave away her entire collection of ancient Celtic heads – which was her life's work, in essence. She could not bear to have any of them around her, after what she had been through. Dr. Ross believed she had come under the influence of an ancient curse. She told researcher Paul Devereux, editor at the time of The Ley Hunter magazine, that she had the heads removed from her house because if she did not, she feared the entire break-down of her family! According to Paul Screeton, the northern journalist, she told Devereaux that the heads had been mysteriously buried, but this must have been some time later, because the next person to take possession of the heads was Dr. Robins, the chemist. He arrived at Dr. Ross' house very excited to collect them. However, the moment he placed the heads inside his car, his car failed to start. All the electronics in the car died. Not to be deterred however, he apparently turned around to the back seat, where he had placed the heads, looked directly at them, and said aloud to them "Stop that." All the electronics in his car then came back on and his car started working again. Unphased, he set off to drive home. However, though brave he may have appeared to be at first, given the reputation the Heads now had, it would not be long before he too came to regret his decisions to become custodian of the heads.

Back home, the chemist began to become just as disturbed as his predecessor Dr Ross. He later declared to Screeton, "There was no doubt that any influence the heads possessed came from the girl!" He means the 'girl' stone head, or the 'Hag,' as she had been called, due to her hooked nose and wild bulging eyes. "I felt most uncomfortable sitting there with them looking at me and eventually we turned them around. As we did so, I had the distinct impression that the girl's eyes slid round watching me." One day, upon leaving the house to go out, he said to the heads, "Let's see something when I get back." He was probably tempting fate here. 'Moments later, he re-entered the house having forgotten to take a book with him. Outside, it was fresh and blustering, but in his study where the heads were, the chemist said the atmosphere seemed, "Almost electric, with a stifling breathless quality." 'Attributing the effects to the 'girl' head, he left hurriedly.' Robins too, it seemed, no longer wanted the heads in his house.

The last known handler of the heads was a man called Frank Hyde. He was what's known as a 'Dowser,' and he said he wanted to carry out some "experiments" with the heads. What experiments he carried out, and what results came from these experiments is not known, for the end to this confusing and bizarre tale is yet another enigma; because not only did the heads disappear but so too did the Dowser! Robins the chemist said, "Frank Hyde seemed to have vanished as completely as if he walked into a fairy hill in a folk tale."

The location of the Dowser and the Heads, remains a tantalizing mystery to this day...

I hope you have enjoyed these stories. If you have, perhaps you would be kind enough to leave a Review,

Thank you so much, Steph

Some of these tales can also be heard on my podcast on iTunes: Tales of Mystery Unexplained

https://podcasts.apple.com/ie/podcast/tales-of-mystery-unexplained/id1216208205

https://www.patreon.com/stephyoungpodcast

Other Books by Steph Young: https://www.amazon.com/Steph-Young/e/B00KE8B6B0/

Tales of Mystery Unexplained

Twisted Tales of Mystery Unexplained

Something in The Woods is Taking People

You can't escape The Woods

Tales for After-Dark: True Ghost Stories

Please go to StephYoungAuthor.com if you would like to stay up to date with new releases.

You can also find me here:

Facebook

Instagram

Twitter

https://podcasts.apple.com/ie/podcast/tales-of-mystery-unexplained/id1216208205

I hope you have enjoyed this book. If you have enjoyed it, perhaps you would be kind enough to leave a Review,

Thank you so much, Steph

Printed in Great Britain
by Amazon